Wishing you
all you may
need for your
journey

Sincerely,

"Greg offers a loving and effective roadmap for getting through hardship, complete with tools for the trip. Not only that, his book gives all of us insights for a meaningful, vital life…"

-From the foreword by *New York Times* bestselling author, Anita Moorjani

JOURNEY BEYOND HARDSHIP:

A Practical, Hopeful Guide For Getting Through Tough Times

GREG PACINI, MS, LPC, CGP

Foreword by *New York Times*
bestselling author, Anita Moorjani

BALBOA.
PRESS
A DIVISION OF HAY HOUSE

Balboa Press books may be ordered through booksellers or by contacting:

Balboa Press
A Division of Hay House
1663 Liberty Drive
Bloomington, IN 47403
www.balboapress.com
1 (877) 407-4847

Print information available on the last page.

ISBN: 978-1-5043-2910-1 (sc)
ISBN: 978-1-5043-2912-5 (hc)
ISBN: 978-1-5043-2911-8 (e)

Library of Congress Control Number: 2015903368

Balboa Press rev. date: 04/10/2015

To Dad and Jean and all who've gone before, with love.

Contents

Acknowledgments

My thanks to all who allowed me into your traumas and tragedies and hardships. Your journeys, with all the pain and all the hurt and all the strength and all the hope, changed me for good. Without your journeys this book would not be.

Thanks to Sophia Rose Cook for your heartfelt, expert, thorough and conscientious editing.

Thanks to Elizabeth Crane for your unfaltering and enthusiastic support of this work, and your willingness to push for the book's expanded direction.

Thank you to the author of the account offered in the final chapter. Thank you for the courage to share your experience and for all that it teaches us.

Thanks to Sandy Shriver for being the consummate professional.

Thank you, Larry Dossey, MD, for your foresight and insight; for being a change agent in the physician training system; for your kindness and your support of this work.

Lastly, thank you Anita Moorjani for the light you brought back to the world and the power it took to endure your hardship. And thank you for gracing this book with the vote of confidence provided by your foreword.

Foreword

I n today's world, it seems like everyone at some time or another will know hardship, whether it's abuse, grief, illness, prejudice, heartbreak, terrorism, addiction, unemployment or natural disaster.

During the hardship I suffered with the diagnosis of my dear friend, Soni, and then with my own illness, family and friends suffered beside me. Our connection to one another made all the difference. But in times of tragedy and trauma, the road gets rough. And while the majority of us will encounter hardship, most of us don't feel prepared for it.

When hardship strikes, I'm sure many wish there was some kind of manual for getting past those challenging times. *Journey Beyond Hardship* is that guide. It offers practical approaches, nourishing advice, and understanding for anyone personally or professionally exposed to hardship, all wrapped in a message of grounded hope.

Using the allegory of a long drive, Greg guides us on a compassionate journey through and beyond the experience of life tragedy or struggle. Sharing compelling stories based on his 35 years as a psychotherapist, Greg takes us from the start of the hardship trip where we leave the familiar. Then he leads us through the detours and potholes along the way, ending beyond the tough times with an exploration of hope, rooted in science.

As outlined in my book, *Dying To Be Me,* illness put me in a coma. And though my body was on the very edge of death, the truest part of me lived on. During that time I had a near death experience (NDE). My NDE taught me many things. Perhaps most importantly, it showed me there is no reason to be afraid.

That powerful near-death event made it unmistakably clear; love beyond our wildest imaginations is waiting completely for us in every minute. As we open to that love, fear falls away—it no longer finds a home in us. Greg's treatment of fear and the power of love, expressed with a strong, relaxed style, makes it evident that his life and his work have taught him some of the very same lessons.

A second important lesson brought by my NDE was that self-love is our natural state. My childhood was rich with diversity, love, and community. However, other factors fostered self-doubt. As a result, in becoming an adult, life was often more about being who I was expected to be, and less about who I wanted to be.

Throughout *Journey Beyond Hardship* we are gently reminded to look kindly on ourselves, just the way we are. Greg not only broadens our awareness of the healing effects of self-love: he tours very specific ways we can expand this essential way of living. And to help as we travel, Greg provides step-by-step techniques for dealing with road blocks and traffic jams like overwhelming emotions, strained relationships, depression and sleeplessness, among others.

Greg offers a loving and effective roadmap for getting through hardship, complete with tools for the trip. Not only that, his book gives all of us insights for a meaningful, vital life, as he speaks from his extensive experience as a psychotherapist. I am certain that any one who reads this book or delves into his work will benefit tremendously from his insights, wisdom, encouragement, as well as from many of the helpful methods he has shared within the pages of this book.

It is my hope that you will come to appreciate Greg's important work as much as I have!

Anita Moorjani

New York Times bestselling author of *"Dying to be Me: My Journey from Cancer, to Near Death, to True Healing"*

Introduction

Hardship is not for the faint of heart. It impacts our sense of self, affects our relationships, and challenges our understanding of what it means to be alive. If something continues to be hard for you, then it is hardship.

You may be lost in the pain of your spouse's death. You may be fighting with all your might to leave an abusive relationship or to recover from an addiction. Your body may be altered by illness or injury, and the adjustment may seem more than you can bear. Miscarriage may have you mourning more than you imagined possible. You may be picking up the pieces of your life after a natural disaster. You may be heartbroken. You may be a target of prejudice. You may be in terror at the news of a diagnosis. You may be struggling after months without work.

Your life may feel empty for some clear reason or no reason at all. You may not have suffered trauma, but you still feel afraid, angry, sad, overburdened or confused about being a single parent, about retirement or simply about being unhappy.

No matter the source, the pain of hardship is scary. Mostly, you just want it to be over. But that's the thing about hardship. It's not just over. It lingers. Given the force of your pain, the desire to stop the uncomfortableness dominates your attention. You tire of the exhaustion and look for a way out.

The way out of hardship, as much as you'd like it to be over, is in and through. In and through is the most direct path to healing. Relief comes sooner. In essence, *Journey Beyond Hardship* is a roadmap to feeling vital; a roadmap to full living.

The early chapters of the book describe how hardship survivors react to the crushing emotions typical of the beginning of the healing journey. These reactions include feeling overwhelmed and immobilized or not feeling anything at all.

The central chapters of the book offer concrete tools for responding to and regulating difficult emotions that eventually, and understandably, surface during hardship. Emotions such as depression, anxiety and anger. One tool, called *Reading the Edges*, helps you recognize the beginning, middle, and end of a feeling, so you can learn to experience the feeling, but not be overcome by it. Without a way to manage your emotions, your emotions manage you. Emotional self-mastery feels good when everything else seems out of control.

In time and with practice using the tools provided, you will gain strength. At that point, you will begin to see beyond your hardship. The final chapters of the book support you there, offering specific guidance for restoring your sense of self and developing hope.

Hardship is part of the human condition. So is the human spirit to overcome.

CHAPTER ONE

Packing: Preparing for The Journey

The Healing Journey

Consider, if you will, your hardship as a journey. The beginning of that journey may be very clear to you though the end seems out of sight. The journey might have started years ago—or just yesterday. You may have had time to prepare for the difficulties of that journey or no time at all. You might have been absolutely overwhelmed when the journey began. Or you may have neatly folded up all your feeling, bundled them away, and carried on.

While we can't take the hardship out of humanity, humanity is equipped with an instinct for healing and wholeness. That instinct just seems broken sometimes. And strange as it may sound, the road to healing goes right through hardship, not around.

As you embark on your journey, please be mindful of this: Compassion is the best fuel. Without the highest possible regard for yourself during this time, your pain will grow. If you get angry, anxious or depressed, and then judge yourself for those reactions, your hardship will be amplified. The truth is, if you tended to be angry, anxious or depressed before the hardship, there's a good chance the stress of your trauma will exaggerate those emotions. Compassion for yourself, right now, as you are, will help the pain. You are allowed to be human.

Beginning the Journey

At the beginning of the journey beyond tragedy, horror, joblessness, a diagnosis, an intense divorce, debt, isolation, betrayal, pain, sleeplessness, abuse, alcohol or rage, you may not even be sure of your destination. Actually, that can be a good thing. Sometimes, when you're not sure where you're going, you increase the chances of arriving somewhere different from where you've always been.

For most, hardship begins with a rush of unbearable feelings. Then, one of four things happens. Some people, in spite of the intense emotions, move on. They just take the next step, and then the next. For others, the highly intense emotions take hold and immobilize them. Still others do something with those powerful, difficult feelings called *packing*. That is, the feelings are so strong and life so demanding they just stop feeling altogether, packing their feelings away. Lastly, many people go forward with their lives, managing some combination of these reactions. All in all, the beginning of the journey is mighty gritty and troublesome. While it's true that good can be found anywhere, hardship by its nature makes good hard to find.

How did your hardship journey begin? Did you have time to prepare? You may have had a quiet sense of knowing that hardship was nearing. Consequently, there may have been time to get ready. Or maybe your hardship came out of nowhere, and in an instant, the world was a very different place.

Were you one of those with a gut feeling that your life was about to change? Deep inside, you may have been putting together small cues or subtle intuitions. For you, when the crippling news came of your hardship, you were stunned, maybe even broken, but not surprised. Perhaps your tragic news came as soldiers knocking on your door, somberly delivering confirmation of fears about your son or daughter in an overseas war. Or it could be, your hardship began with devastating lab results that validated an instinct about your unborn child.

Perhaps for you, the inner rumblings that kept you up at night were proven right when your spouse walked away from the dinner table saying, "I'm in love with someone else." Or the hardship may have begun for you as all the pieces fell uncomfortably into place with the announcement at a staff meeting of major job cuts.

On the other hand, your hardship may have come with no time for you to prepare. Many life traumas arrive with no warning: a phone call informs you of the accidental death of your spouse; a normal day at work becomes something very different when a machine malfunction takes your sight; a routine colonoscopy quickly becomes anything but routine when you awake to the news of a cancer diagnosis; a walk to your car at the mall turns into a horrific violation in the parking lot; a scream from next-door calls you to the aid of a neighbor whose spouse had committed suicide; a natural disaster leveled your home in a matter of minutes. In these cases, nothing hints at the start of the hardship journey.

Packing for the Journey

Whether your hardship unfolded with warning or with no notice at all, in the beginning of the journey, things change drastically, and it's challenging to keep pace. You can feel sick on emotion. You can't catch up with yourself. On top of your emotional upheaval, there are often many urgent practical matters needing attention. As a result, painful thoughts and feelings can take a back seat. It's OK.

This is *packing*: tucking away difficult images and emotions that can flood you at the beginning of the journey beyond hardship. Packing affords you the energy and focus needed for daily life.

Just like preparing for a trip, packing in this sense can be a way to get ready for the journey ahead. Packing can steady you emotionally, mentally or relationally for the coming days, months or even years on the hardship road.

This is a strained, strange and unstable stage of the journey. The mind whirls. The body suffers. The heart aches. And yet in this most vulnerable time, you're asked to keep functioning in the world because the world keeps going with its jobs and responsibilities and demands for your time.

In those early weeks of your journey, did you feel lost? Did you wish you had a map? Did you wonder who was driving? Did you hope it wasn't you? Maybe you felt a surge of sureness about your travels. Perhaps you felt a rush of certainty and strength, deeply aware of what was being called for at this moment in your life. Too, you may have felt a shift in the way you viewed the people you care about. Maybe you started to act differently with them—more loving or more distant.

Perhaps you felt terribly alone. Maybe you found a trusted person you could talk to about your fear, your terror.

You may have rallied your faith in something or someone, or just sat and wondered. You may have fought wave after wave of feeling, or perhaps you stepped out of that ocean altogether. Maybe you caught yourself spending hours on the Internet looking for answers or direction. Perhaps you asked cloaked questions of family, friends or professionals, testing some sixth sense against a harder reality.

In preparing, you may have withdrawn from your usual ways, or maybe you noticed yourself racing. Could be, you began to pack away your hope. Did you box up your fear, confusion, disillusionment, anger, or sadness? Did you pack for your family?

At the start, it's often just about the next step: arrangements to be made, appointments to set and keep, emergency management, loved ones to see, insurance companies to call. Then more follow up. Consequently, you may have bypassed part or all of the initial emotions, knowing your strength was needed to contend with all this external activity.

What do people do with the bouts of sorrow, fear, hurt and more that can come at the beginning of the journey? Some pack those feelings away. Others say to themselves, "I can do this, I've handled worse." Others collapse quietly alone somewhere. Some cry. Some die inside for a minute. Some, way down in there someplace, whisper, "Why me?" Others proclaim, "Why not me!?" Many seek comfort in an explanation. Others pray. Some push others out of the way and say, "Let me do the driving." Still others make absolutely certain that their circle of support is in place.

Additionally, some experience shame: "I brought this on with my own hectic life," or, "I should have seen this coming." Others feel blame: "If it weren't for you, things would be different," or, "How could God let this happen?" And still others stuff all the courage, trust, love, confidence, and peace they can possibly fit in their emotional suitcase.

Some lives stop altogether when hardship hits: too much to feel, too much to see, too much to hear. Each reaction has its place. None is better than the other.

Later, you will unpack from your journey. But packing is typical and often necessary in the beginning. Now it's time to leave home.

CHAPTER TWO

Leaving Home—The Familiar

Leaving The Familiar Behind

As with most trips, on the journey through hardship once the packing is finished, you leave home. And what is home? Home is where you dangle your legs from the kitchen counter late at night, eating a cold piece of chicken while your spouse snacks on homemade coffee cake. When life is good, home is a place of comfort, peace, passion, acceptance, and familiarity. Home is a place you know.

When the journey beyond hardship begins, you leave the familiar. You leave the comfort of a well-known way of life for a place about which you know little. When you leave this metaphorical home, this place of comfort, what else is left behind? Some leave behind a fear they've lived with all their lives. Others, especially in the beginning, leave their peace and hope. Some leave the rocky road of personal issues. Like magic, tragedy can lift years of marital discord or tension within a family, as all unite to take on the trauma. Others leave shaky relationships outright, trusting such decisions will make them feel better and enable them to take on the challenge life has served up. Still others find a deeper connection to themselves.

Leaving Parts of the Personality

Jeff was thirty-nine years old when his wife died suddenly of a heart attack. The sudden loss left him adrift. As if the grief weren't enough, Jeff, a nurse, battled deep feelings of guilt about not recognizing his wife's symptoms. But most of the guilt was tucked away because he was consumed with his role as the sole caretaker of three children.

Jeff began counseling about ten months after his wife's death. Jeff had been professionally taking care of people all his adult life. When immersed in the experience of letting others help him, especially when it came to the children, Jeff realized something.

Pushing past uncomfortable emotions he revealed, "I wouldn't wish this situation on anybody. But it's changed me. I've spent all my life caring for others. When Sharon's death forced me to surrender to being cared for by others, I felt a sort of melting in me. I didn't understand it at first. Actually, I resisted it," Jeff said.

When I invited him to explain, Jeff continued, "I resisted letting others help me out. It's not something I've really ever had a lot of. But once I let go to that help, it was like medicine to me. That's when I realized that being cared for was what I wanted."

Jeff finished emphatically, "All these years of caring for others, I've been giving what I've always wanted to get."

Jeff's hardship helped him leave the safe ground of always serving others. Being served can be very unnerving for a caregiver. Jeff's strength allowed the tragedy to teach him, and his emotional life eventually improved. This can happen when we leave the familiar.

Leaving Relationships In Subtle Ways

Others traveling the journey beyond hardship find themselves leaving well-worn ways of relating to immediate family members. Karen was twenty-seven when her doctor said, "Your white cell counts are very elevated. Further testing is needed, but it's most likely you have leukemia. I'm sorry."

Three or four sessions into our work together after the diagnosis, Karen reported a change in how she was acting with her two daughters.

"I'm finding things to do on the weekends so I don't have to be at home with the girls," Karen shared. When I asked her about these choices with her girls she explained, "I think it helps me to just stay busy, but I'm not sure. The whole thing scares me."

I suggested that she consider listening to what was going on inside the next few times she made plans that didn't include her daughters. Identifying those feelings in the moment could help her understand her actions.

It wasn't long before Karen began to unpeel her emotions about the changing relationship with her daughters. Yes, staying busy did help her. Then she realized that there was a pain under the busyness. The pain was strongest around her girls. Eventually, she discovered a collision between her love for her daughters and the fear of something happening to herself. She was unconsciously leaving

9

her children a little bit at a time, to lessen the blow of the permanent separation she feared.

In time, Karen also uncovered at an even deeper level something that surprised her. She felt a tinge of jealousy for the exuberance and carefree ways of people she saw in public places like malls and schoolyards. She even admitted some of this same jealousy for her life-loving daughters. Driven by all these feelings, Karen had left home: left the more familiar, connected relationship she had with her children prior to the diagnosis.

Other Ways of Leaving the Familiar

Like Karen, many traveling the hardship road find it difficult to be around happy people. Happiness seems to be in the rear view mirror and getting farther away.

Others move away from believing they are part of the "normal" world. Some say goodbye to their sense of invincibility. Some pull away from their spirituality. Many part with a feeling of control about life. For many, independence and self-assurance seem like they've been left behind.

Finally, some disconnect from a mind that can sometimes be still, concentrate, or remember. They disconnect from a deep knowing that A plus B does equal C. And those closest to the person dealing with hardship detach from many of the very same things—sometimes more.

Leaving things behind at this point in the journey is really the experience of loss, and loss brings its own set of feelings. But with so much external activity at the start of the journey beyond, this loss often goes unnoticed. When intense emotions overwhelm us, it may feel like we've lost ourselves.

It's important to remember that leaving home is just a beginning. Leaving something behind doesn't mean you can't return to it later.

CHAPTER THREE

On The Road: Beginning the Recovery Process

We're Not in Kansas Anymore

"There's no place like home. There's no place like home." Comfort is a common wish as the journey unfolds, but hardship takes us to unfamiliar lands. Whether your hardship has been the loss of a loved one, relocation, financial downfall, fending off addiction or some other difficulty, life is not the same. More importantly, going forward may mean driving through some very rough terrain: lifestyle modifications, moving, mourning, rehabilitation, repairing the relationship with yourself and others. Getting up the steam needed to head down the road may seem hard to do.

How do you begin to move forward from the confounding and unearthing experiences that make up life hardships? To be sure, there is no formula. We fumble and stumble at times just to stay upright. Sometimes even that seems like a tall order.

Those who got back on track relatively quickly after a life tragedy are fortunate. If, however, you're having a hard time regaining your balance after a hardship, here's a look at some fundamentals that may help you move in the direction you want.

Your Approach

Traveling down the road after tragedy can feel like driving in the dark with your headlights off. In part, this is because of changes inside you. Your life was moving along nicely, or, at the very least, you were finding your way around the life you called your own. Then, hardship rearranged all that. As a result, you may not feel sure of who you are anymore or how to make your way. What once made sense to you really doesn't now; it's as if your compass is broken.

At times like this, an approach to life can operate as a kind of GPS. A guiding principle can stabilize your goings and comings. However, you may feel tragedy shattered your guiding principle. You may not know what you believe anymore.

Some of the guiding principles people question after tragedy: "It'll all work out in the end," "It's in God's hands," and the ever-popular, "Life only gives you as much as you can handle."

If your guiding principle no longer sustains you, what then?

What You Believe About Living

If you pay attention, you'll begin to notice what it is you do believe. Your actions reflect those beliefs and so do the thoughts in your head.

13

Your thoughts may be saying, "This is a waste. What am I doing here? None of this makes sense." There is absolutely nothing wrong with those thoughts. Nothing. At the same time, repeating those thoughts again and again will steal your energy.

Or your thoughts may be saying, "There's not one damn thing about this that I get. I don't know how I'm gonna go on, but…I guess I am." Now there's nothing particularly correct or righteous about these thoughts. However, these kinds of thoughts may actually give you some energy, rather than take it away.

It's that simple. Some thoughts give life. Other thoughts take life. With closer inspection you will begin to notice whether your thoughts are slowly giving you life or slowly taking it away. Once you become conscious about this, you begin to either choose life or choose it's opposite. This isn't about good or bad, right or wrong. It's about how you're feeling in the life you have.

Healing is not a straight line. Some days your thoughts can seem to be lifting you, and other days your thoughts may seem to be pulling you down. But if you track the course of your life-giving or life-taking thoughts over time, the trajectory is generally heading up or heading down.

Choice is the bottom line. Do you want your life course heading up…or heading down? As crazy as it sounds, the question becomes, "Do you want your life to feel better?" No one else can decide this. Friends can impact us. Professionals can help. But when all is said and done, each of us decides the quality of our next minute, our next week, year and life. To be sure, this simple choice can be desperately painful.

Folks who choose the, "I–don't–know–what–I'm–gonna–do–about–all–this, but–here–I–go," way of thinking stir a little strength in their minds and emotions and bodies. And those with the, "What's–the–point?" thoughts stir a little weakening. This is not just a dramatic statement—it is science.[1]

Making choices about your life is not a moral issue, but a factual one. Each of us makes choices, moment to moment. Those moments add up. What, fundamentally, is taking place? The self *is* establishing an approach for life; a go-forward, hit-neutral, back-up or stop approach for living. Looked at from another angle, this is powerful creation. Each of us gets to create the kind of experience we want.

Because this one choice that we each make all the time can be the single most important ingredient in the quality of our lives, it's worth becoming aware of just exactly what it is that you choose. Put differently, each of us, knowingly or not, has an approach to life. By being more conscious, we can determine if we like the approach we're living by. If we don't like it, we can change it up. Just how to change it up we explore later. And changing it up early in the journey beyond hardship may be hard indeed.

Relationships Can Assist Us on Our Journey

When making the hardship journey, many find it helpful to have travel companions. Science also tells us that people who maintain connections usually get through tough times better.[2] These connections could be with friends, family members, church or civic groups, helping professionals, and even pets.

When we connect and let others in, what helps us most is their compassion, openness, presence, humor, strength and clarity. The strength of others helps us to find our own. Compassion from others helps us have compassion for ourselves. Humor changes our chemistry and makes us feel better for a bit. And the openness of others allows us to be open to ourselves and all that can surface from our inner states that we may have never visited.

But relationships are curious creatures. Some people feel they get a shot of energy when they are with family or friends. Others feel they lose energy around people. This, by some standards, defines the extrovert and the introvert.

While you may generally be a more social person, when you're in pain, you may like to be left alone. On the road beyond hardship, you may find yourself overwhelmed by others and their feelings about your situation. Even the support of others can sometimes take you to emotional places you'd rather not go in that moment. Staying to yourself at times like that is an example of what we might call *emotional efficiency.*

Having said that, it does seem true that most people feel some lift after visiting, texting, Skyping, hugging, Instagramming or e-mailing someone they care about, especially when things are tough.

Relationships May Change During the Journey

Just as relationships are important during the journey beyond hardship, so are changes in those relationships. Eric's forty-year-old daughter was held at gunpoint six months earlier. "Some part of me thinks she should just get on with her life. And yet I know she's scared," Eric expressed. "I don't really know what's best for her. Should I push her or hold her?"

These are the questions of people trying to find their place in someone else's journey, not unlike the turning and twisting that happens in the car during long drives. Relationships shift and turn. Everybody tries to figure out how to relate, in light of the hardship: "Will I call a lot or just send cards?"; "Will I ask about the situation or just talk about everyday things?"

When you go on a long drive, everyone is usually wide awake for the first hundred miles. There's a kind of united focus. All are intent on the journey itself. There's talk in the car about where you're going and how you're going to get there.

The same is true with the journey beyond hardship. Trauma usually draws people together with a common goal and united focus. What is typically talked about in the beginning is where you're headed and how you're going to get there. That is, people draw on relationships to do everything possible, in the best way possible, to keep things headed in the right direction.

Safety on the Journey

Right after food, water and shelter on Maslow's Hierarchy of Needs is *safety*. Safety is essential for health, but has an even greater bearing on well being during crisis and hardship. Though safety in its most basic form is physical, we're going to look at psychological safety.

Interestingly enough, psychological safety grows from an approach to living and relationships.

So let's circle back to the issue of a personal approach to living. If we establish an approach with life force in it that suits us, and we live by that approach consciously during hardship, we will feel safer. When questions and doubts surface (and they will), this internal rudder provided by our approach will help us navigate. It's no surprise that in difficult times, the mind gets muddied and manic. A guiding belief or thought system has the effect of settling that mental snow globe. Things appear clearer. When there is clarity, we generally feel safer.

Untold numbers of folks believe in a Higher Self or God or that everything happens for a reason. Unlike some who lose connection to previously held ideals, these people hold even more tightly to their beliefs during hardship. Their guiding principle feels profoundly safe to them.

The issue is less about what you believe and more about that you believe. So, even if you believe, "There's nothing to believe in. I just have to get up and do this,"—that becomes your guiding principle and it will help. There is life force. There is a sense of safety within from that belief choice.

To the contrary, choosing to believe, "There's nothing to believe in. Why do this?" repeats a pattern of thoughts that is without life force and will give rise to something in you that does not feel safe. Granted, anyone on the journey beyond hardship may have these hopeless thoughts on occasion. But it's when hopeless thoughts become a belief system, a way of being in the world, that we stop feeling safe. Without some modicum of safety, going through hardship is tough going, indeed.

Psychological safety is generated from the inside out, based in part on what approach to living we've chosen. However, relationships can affect our sense of safety, too. Fundamentally, good relationships can provide a feeling of safety when we can't manufacture it ourselves. In this way, healthy relationships can bridge an emotional gap in our sense of safety during times of hardship.

For some, though, relationships do not feel safe. Feelings of safety and security develop in humans when important people in our early lives are there for us in healthy ways. Sadly, early life situations can compromise the sense of safety a child might feel. This includes abuse, neglect, or chemical dependency by a parent, relative, neighbor or significant other. Then there are those less obvious circumstances in a child's life that may compromise safety: multiple relocations, a parent who travels or is away from the home a lot, bullying siblings, an ill parent, or a parent whose emotional needs supersede the child's. In each of these scenarios, the child still naturally wants to connect to the parent or parental figure, but the situation makes that connection difficult to establish.

When a child feels deeply connected to the important figures in his or her life, that child feels safe. More importantly, those formative connections foster the child's ability to connect deeply to him or herself. The child then grows up to feel safe in the world, because he or she feels safe inside, connected to self. Relationships for that child felt nourishing. Therefore, the child develops into an adult who feels drawn to connect deeply to others.

Having been nourished in this way as a young one, the child becomes an adult capable of loving and being loved. The adult who experiences formative connections, later connects to the experience of being a human—to being alive. These factors make the healthy adult more likely to choose the, "I-don't-get-this, but-I-just-need-to-take-the-next-step," approach. In other words, when we are loved, we better love ourselves and life, we feel safer in the world, and we are better equipped to make it through when hardship finds us.

But if early life circumstances compromised our connections to the important adults in our young lives, we may struggle now to connect with ourselves, others and life itself. We don't feel safe. So when tragedy strikes, we are less likely to reach out to others, and getting through seems almost impossible. Then some part of us says, "What's the point. I can't do this anymore."

If you feel alone, scared, angry and devastated by hardship; if you don't feel connected to yourself or worse yet, don't like who you are; if there's nothing inside that wants to stay on the road of life, then reaching inside and taking the next step seems awfully hard to do. No one knows that better than you.

What could be happening is that you have no real internal reference for being cared for; you don't know what that feels like. If you're one of those people who never felt good enough as a child, then you probably never truly connected to an important adult figure in a healthy way. In some sense, you were never truly loved just as you are.

As a result, you know more about what it means to want love than to feel love. Instead of being loved, you were taught to be careful and do the things that avoided punishment, or do the things that brought you approval. Approval and love are very different.

So then what?

You're invited to consider whether or not you can let love in. If you can, you will start to feel better. In time, you may actually feel a bit better about yourself. Then it gets easier to let love in from a few more people. That love may give you the steam to take the next step with your life, and then momentum can build, and you may eventually see a reason for being here. You feel safer and so does life. Then you're back on the road.

If you find yourself in the kind of dark place just described, whether or not you can see it, believe it, or realize it in the moment, contact with another person is most helpful right now. Please allow that.

With care from someone else, you can begin to organize inside yourself an approach that is more life affirming, an approach that may make it easier to travel with a sense of safety. Hardship won't seem quite so hard.

CHAPTER FOUR

Refreshments: Little Ways to Take Care of Yourself

A re you one of those folks on road trips who digs into the chocolates or those organic blue corn tortilla chips before you even leave the driveway? On the journey beyond hardship, it's a good idea to hit the refreshments of the heart early and often. Snacking on certain kinds of refreshments helps revive the spirit and maintain focus. It's an understatement that this journey can drain you. Without attention to those activities that return energy, strength, focus, and motivation, travelers may find it difficult to finish the trip.

So here's an opportunity, by looking over the menu of "snacks" below, to check your cooler and see how you're doing when it comes to maintaining your strength:

- ☐ Study the stars
- ☐ Cut the grass
- ☐ Listen to laughter
- ☐ Walk to the mailbox

- ☐ Make cookies
- ☐ Write a letter
- ☐ Study the faces of those you love
- ☐ Tenderly tickle a child
- ☐ Volunteer
- ☐ Just sit
- ☐ Work on your car
- ☐ Knit
- ☐ Play catch
- ☐ Play poker
- ☐ Read
- ☐ Go to your counselor
- ☐ Talk with your nurse
- ☐ Talk with another hardship survivor
- ☐ Sing in the wind
- ☐ Burn sage
- ☐ Practice your violin
- ☐ Dance in the snow
- ☐ Fiddle
- ☐ Paint
- ☐ Dance in the arms of someone you love
- ☐ Work a crossword puzzle
- ☐ Pat your dog on the head
- ☐ Kiss your baby's cheek
- ☐ Crank up the music
- ☐ Hold your lover closer than you ever have
- ☐ Lay in the sun

- ☐ Call your grandfather
- ☐ Look through old pictures
- ☐ Take new ones
- ☐ Look soulfully at your life
- ☐ Share your thoughts with someone you trust
- ☐ Break sticks and yell
- ☐ Go to a farm and talk to the horses
- ☐ Hit the gym
- ☐ Have a beer
- ☐ Write a letter to someone you respect, with your weaker hand
- ☐ Cut out magazine pictures that remind you of you and give them to your mate
- ☐ Drum
- ☐ Sit on the floor and have a sandwich with a kiddo
- ☐ Notice how your hands work
- ☐ Turn off your phone
- ☐ Close your Twitter account
- ☐ Open one
- ☐ Ask someone to help you
- ☐ Help someone
- ☐ Fly in your mind
- ☐ Stand with your feet in the sand
- ☐ Collect rocks that mean something to you
- ☐ Lie flat on your back but not in your bed
- ☐ Color
- ☐ Throw darts
- ☐ Throw a football

- ☐ Throw a party tomorrow
- ☐ Throw out the junk in your house
- ☐ Throw your arms around somebody
- ☐ Throw a fit
- ☐ Throw your cares to the wind and see where they land
- ☐ Live for a day as if you were somebody else
- ☐ Learn from it
- ☐ Teach somebody what you learned
- ☐ Learn to love something new
- ☐ Make up a song and sing it in the shower
- ☐ Shower with your clothes on
- ☐ Invite your lover in to take them off
- ☐ Turn the lights off and watch the darkness
- ☐ Talk to the darkness
- ☐ Speak of the light
- ☐ Listen
- ☐ Love every part of yourself
- ☐ Tell the truth
- ☐ Own what you don't particularly care for about you
- ☐ Confess
- ☐ Believe in something important
- ☐ Write about those beliefs
- ☐ Write a book
- ☐ Date your wife
- ☐ Dazzle somebody, without words
- ☐ Wait at the door for something wonderful to arrive and pretend it gets there

- ☐ Deliver an important message to the world driving home
- ☐ Clap your hands for the hell of it
- ☐ Take a bow while you're at it
- ☐ Ride a train
- ☐ Ride off into the sunset for somebody
- ☐ Tap your fingers
- ☐ Tape a note on your own back that tells people what you need today
- ☐ Smell something new
- ☐ Feed the birds
- ☐ Burn a candle as a gesture of respect
- ☐ Take back your power
- ☐ Gather up something wonderful in your arms
- ☐ Donate
- ☐ Take some time for trimming your nails
- ☐ Be on time
- ☐ Be late
- ☐ Be proud of who you are
- ☐ Be silly
- ☐ Be bold
- ☐ Be wrong
- ☐ Be right
- ☐ Be alone
- ☐ Be surrounded by people who love you
- ☐ Be yourself again
- ☐ Be afraid of nothing for seven minutes
- ☐ Be that person you used to be if only in your mind

☐ Be very appreciative of who you've become

☐ Be kind

☐ Belong to something

☐ Be careful

☐ Be carefree

☐ Be the apple of someone's eye and ask them to be the same for you

☐ Be that ten-year-old boy

☐ Be stillness

☐ Pay for someone's dinner without them knowing

☐ Bring home flowers even if you're the only one there

☐ Hold your breath and listen to your own heart beat

☐ Hold your purse on the other arm

☐ Hold hands for a long, long time

☐ Hold back; let it go

☐ Hold something very precious for just a second

☐ Hold a meeting and let everybody know how you want to do this, whatever this is

☐ Have a piece of fruit, but make each bite last fifteen seconds

☐ Do some chocolate

☐ Bake a cake from scratch

☐ Carry a piece of chopped wood

☐ Take a nap

☐ Take another nap

☐ Tell somebody you did

☐ Have them join you

☐ Make a mountain out of a molehill for fun

- ☐ Spell everything backwards
- ☐ Box with your boyfriend
- ☐ Be gentle
- ☐ Be vital if only for that long
- ☐ Give it a try
- ☐ Try it again tomorrow
- ☐ Make a paper airplane
- ☐ Forgive yourself for good
- ☐ Fix a little something
- ☐ Fast, if your doctor thinks it's OK
- ☐ If you can't fast, give something up
- ☐ Celebrate being sober
- ☐ Be more powerful than you ever have
- ☐ Let your eyes tear up
- ☐ Touch someone's lips with your own
- ☐ Watch a stupid movie
- ☐ Take five every time you can
- ☐ Work hard and feel the rich joy
- ☐ Pat somebody on the back in a way that really touches them, you know, mean it
- ☐ Be kind with it
- ☐ Think about the moon
- ☐ Forgive anybody you want
- ☐ Cover your plants when it gets cold
- ☐ Let your children know you can be loving *and* strong
- ☐ Carry through with it
- ☐ Tackle something

☐ Wave

☐ Have a banana split

☐ Have a cow

☐ Don't stop noticing

☐ Count your blessings as contrived as that might seem

☐ Rub some brown, crackly leaves in your hands

☐ Let your palms just barely touch the tips of new grass blades

☐ Hear your lover's voice, not the words

☐ Cuddle

☐ Splash in a puddle

☐ Find someplace to watch deer

☐ Tiptoe, trying not to wake

☐ Feel your heart—the emotional part—when saying goodbye to someone

☐ Goof around

☐ Remember who you are

Does anything jump out at you when you read this list? It might be worth paying attention to. It might be worth reading again in a week, to see if your reaction shifts. The shift might be worth paying attention to.

If you're up for more than a snack, take a minute to consider these questions: How do you care for yourself when you feel stressed?

What do you do when you're not stressed to prevent becoming stressed?

What do you do that ignites your spirit?

What makes you feel loved?

What makes you feel loving?

What brings you much gratitude?

Where, when, and how do you find your peace?

When you need comfort, how do you get it?

Who are the people you feel best around?

CHAPTER FIVE

Unpacking: Thoughts About Tough Feelings

During the journey beyond, there may be times of intense relief and joy, times of utter loss and confusion, times of profound faith and strength, or times of despair and disbelief. Some emotions may be more poignant than others, some more pervasive, others more enduring. But in the beginning of the trip, many feelings can get packed away, especially if they're difficult.

According to an article in *Social Science and Medicine*, chronic physical conditions can bring on depression and put a dent in self esteem.[3] Makes sense that at the start of the journey beyond all kinds of hardship, you are stuffed full of emotions.

However, there's only so much you can jam in your emotional suitcase. Unless you unpack some of these tough feelings, psychological pressure will cause you to live in emotional extremes. You'll find yourself having outbursts, withdrawals, tears, and complete shutdowns. These responses are not wrong. However, the ride can be very rough when journeying on these severe emotional reactions alone.

What's called for is a broader range of feelings. Here's how it works. Early in the journey, there was a wide and powerful spectrum of emotions coursing through you. Eventually, those emotions interfered with the requirements of daily life, so they got packed. But when demands created by the tragedy cleared and there was a little room to breathe, you started to recover strength. It's this strength that then allows you to venture into the emotions you didn't have time or energy to feel early on. When you begin to experience the broader spectrum of emotions, and not just the extremes described above, you are *unpacking*.

When you unpack, you stop holding feelings in. When you stop holding feelings in, you release emotional pressure. When you release emotional pressure, your system doesn't need to decompress through extreme reactions. Now the road is smoothing out.

Feelings: Right or Wrong?

Feelings such as sadness, fear, anger and disappointment historically have been described as negative. Yet, all emotions are positive when we think of each as a signpost pointing to what works for us and what doesn't.

All emotions teach. If we only read the signposts of positive emotions, we'll get lost, because some of the most important guidance we receive is from the more difficult feelings. For instance, if someone continues making you the butt of their jokes after you've asked them to stop, your sadness or anger is an essential signpost guiding you to a healthy response.

It is only natural to experience all kinds of emotions during hardship. Giving yourself permission to honor these feelings as they occur is part of an authentic experience. Unfortunately, having an authentic experience is sometimes misinterpreted as having a bad attitude. Consequently, many on the hardship road find themselves contending with more than their tragedy. They find themselves also wrestling with the opinions of people who insist they stay positive. As a result, hardship travelers wind up confused, because their tough feelings are very real. Yet people who love them often suggest they not feel those harder emotions.

Word on the street is, "Positive attitude is everything." The fact is, when on a journey beyond hardship being positive can help. A study cited in *Stress: The International Journal on the Biology of Stress* reports that people who received six weeks of training in visualization, (seeing themselves well) "up-regulated" or strengthened their immune systems.[4] The visualizations worked.

Additionally, an article in *Seminars in Clinical Neuropsychiatry* reports that hypnotic-like methods involving relaxation, suggestion, and imagery have a significant impact on pain.[5] Attitude and the mind can have a positive influence.

But positive is not always what you feel on the journey beyond hardship. Tough feelings do surface and the process of going through the harder feelings may have a different kind of positive impact.

I had the good fortune to hear David Spiegel, MD, of Stanford University, speak at a luncheon. Dr. Spiegel's work with cancer survivors was featured on Bill Moyers's PBS series, *Healing and the Mind*. His luncheon message was clear: Always being positive is a misguided response when confronted with illness. In other words, *going through* some of the tough feelings may help.

This message may leave you with questions: "Am I going to hurt myself or derail my progress if I'm not positive, and let myself feel sad, angry, disappointed or confused?" "Will letting myself have this broader range of emotions work against me?"

Rollin McCraty, Ph.D., Executive Vice President and Director of Research at the Institute for HeartMath, stated that, "People who maintain an inner feeling of anger in the form of a slow burn actually extend the suppression of their immune system." [6] That means holding in anger is costly.

Furthermore, research says the suppression or avoidance of emotional material not only interferes with learning and maintains anxiety, but may also *increase* anxiety and impede overall emotional health.[7]

The research suggests that pushing away or holding down difficult emotions is hard on us. This pushing away is essentially the same thing as packing. Unpacking is a good idea according to science.

Learning to Unpack

Audrey had a lot to unpack. Not only did she find the strength to do just that, she also found a better life on the other side of unpacking.

Audrey had been doing her best to create a new life after a freak car accident had taken her right leg just below the knee. Before her accident, Audrey was very active with full-time employment and a family. She enjoyed hiking and runs through the woods with her dog.

Audrey's early journey in psychotherapy focused on anger and sadness. These feelings came in alternating waves. Then she began to consciously grieve. She mourned the loss of her limb first. Next, Audrey grieved all the less obvious losses that often come with losing some part of the body: loss of physical freedom, loss of body image, loss of independence, loss of dreams, loss of esteem, loss of favorite activities and clothes, and more. Audrey even lost a familiar gait, stance, and posture. Lots to unpack.

With time, however, Audrey eventually recovered much of the self she felt disconnected from early on. Getting comfortable with a prosthetic leg made a big difference. The sadness and anger began to lift. As her mourning turned to living, and Audrey felt times of real joy again, another set of emotions surfaced that seemed somehow vaguely familiar. More to unpack.

"I've spent thirty-eight years running from one thing to the next," Audrey revealed. "Man, I couldn't stand still. But I get it now. It scares me to death to stand still. If I stand still, I might notice how sad I am."

Audrey and I explored early life experiences that represented another kind of loss that she had never mourned, and the old sadness poured out. Beneath emotions occurring naturally with a difficult event, we find related emotions that are relics of past pain. At times like these, the emotional suitcase may feel like it's going to bust open.

Unpacking some of these feelings may help. It helped Audrey. In time, she and I got to the bottom of her very old sadness rooted in the abuse she suffered as a child. Once the profound hurt connected to that early emotional injury was unpacked, Audrey began to feel alive in a whole new way.

The bottom line, as tough feelings surface during your journey beyond—and they are going to surface—let them move through you. Try not to get stuck in any feeling, but give each its due. This will smooth out your ride. Emotions are important signposts, but not the destination. Churchill said, "If you're going through hell, keep going." Visit the emotional pain, but don't pitch a tent there.

CHAPTER SIX

Rest Stop #1: Triple A—The Simple Tool for Responding to Tough Feelings

D uring any long drive, there are places along the way to take a break. You can either pull off and rest or keep going. The same is true with the healing journey. This chapter, like other Rest Stop chapters, is designed to break up the trip a bit and help you along your way.

With this Rest Stop, you learn the unpacking technique used for managing tough emotions, in general. As you practice unpacking, you develop greater emotional range, which allows you to handle the ups and downs of the road ahead. Like good shock absorbers, greater emotional range keeps you from bottoming out or losing control in dangerous curves.

Here is a three-step technique—Triple A—to help you "unpack" some of the difficult emotions you may be carrying on your journey.

Triple A

Step 1. Acknowledge

Step 2. Accept

Step 3. Act

Step 1. Acknowledge

Until your feelings of sadness, anger, frustration, or confusion are acknowledged, nothing changes. Your discomfort persists. Uncomfortable and persistent feelings that are not identified may go underground. Therese Rando, a noted psychologist, calls this kind of emotional response *avoidance.*[8]

Avoidance seems a negative word. And yet, at times there can be wisdom in avoiding significant, difficult feelings, especially early on. For example, it may be *emotionally efficient* not to talk of a recent tragedy at your daughter's basketball game. Diving into all the emotions in that public place may undo you, and then you have a second trauma, and that would be emotionally <u>in</u>efficient, or costly.

Trouble may brew, however, if tough feelings along the hardship journey are never considered. When feelings go permanently underground, they can manage you rather than you managing them. More often than not these hidden, difficult feelings express themselves through behavior. You may buzz around, trying to stay on the surface of your life, or you may find yourself lethargic because precious energy is spent working to keep unexpressed feelings packed away. Some people have angry outbursts as the hidden feelings build and then release. Some folks become plain snarky, which is often how unacknowledged feelings come out sideways. Some eventually withdraw or shut down the emotional self all together.

The first step in unpacking and preventing the buildup that can lead to emotional bottoming out is to *acknowledge* what is going on inside you: acknowledge that something is out of sync.

To acknowledge that you feel some difficult things somewhere inside is no more than that. This step is not about doing anything with those feelings. It is only about noticing them. The process of noticing is perhaps the simplest but most profound and effective of all the therapeutic tools. Noticing feelings is like having a wise and gentle observer inside. This observer brings no judgment or pressure to change what is noticed. The observer does nothing more than sees what is. And it is this observer who will help you eventually *Read The Edges* of tough emotions, so as to mitigate them. When you Read The Edges of any feeling, you recognize the emotion's beginning, middle and end. This awareness positions you to actually experience that feeling without being overwhelmed by it. It all starts with the simple act of acknowledging.

Step 2. Accept

Acknowledgment of your feelings seems easy enough. Yet, with that seemingly simple gesture, another reaction might be put into motion. You might feel bad about what you notice. Many of us, when we recognize our emotions, immediately feel ashamed, frustrated or disappointed: "I can't believe this still makes me mad", or "When am I gonna stop being afraid?"

That's why Step 2 makes a difference. If you don't *accept* all that you uncover inside, a battle may ensue between who you are and who you think you should be. Acknowledging has nothing to do with should, could, or ought to be. By simply embracing whatever you find inside, the process of going through hardship can continue.

But this kind of unconditional acceptance of you may feel foreign and unusual. So much of our world insists that when something is not "right", there must be accountability or punishment—change, at the very least. With this mindset, the idea of just accepting all that you find inside may feel as if you're not doing enough. By just accepting your feelings, it may seem that you're not going to improve. It might even feel as if accepting feelings is giving them more power.

To the contrary, by acknowledging and accepting all that you feel, those difficult emotions are often disempowered. This can free up much needed energy.

Always holding tough feelings in is a little like putting a dog in your basement—not a particularly friendly dog, but not a mean dog either. If you forget the dog's down there, beware. After a while, when you do go back, there's gonna be a mess. Wait even longer, and the dog could turn on you. All of us and all parts of us need attention.

If you befriend your feelings, they won't get mean. They might even support you. Attending to tough feelings may help prevent them from making a mess inside you or worse, doing some emotional damage. Giving your feelings attention can improve the quality of your life.

There is another benefit from simply acknowledging and accepting your feelings. When you witness and accept feelings, you become an observer of yourself. Consequently, the whole of you is no longer sad or fearful or hopeless. Only a part of you is. So now there's the part of you watching the reaction, and there's the part of you reacting. The part of you watching the reaction is positioned to choose a different reaction.

Essentially, you enter the eye of the storm. In this way it is possible to be quiet within yourself, even in the presence of strong emotions. From this quiet place, choice becomes possible, and that changes everything. Yet when you are simply caught up in emotion, without the witness self, there is only reaction. You and the reaction are one in the same. Choice is then out of the picture.

So, by not doing anything with your feelings beyond *acknowledging* them and *accepting* them, you really are doing something.

However, when you consistently circle around your tough feelings by ignoring them, those feelings stack up, creating a wall between you and a life of genuine joy, strength, courage, and hope. Acknowledging and accepting the bricks of your difficult emotions dismantles the wall, giving you a way through to a more comfortable life.

What does accepting a feeling sound like? If your internal, objective and compassionate observer could speak, it might have this to share about your sadness: "I am sad right now. I could start crying. I know it's because I really need to talk to somebody, but it's too late to call. I accept this sadness." When you look directly at your feelings like this, they move on more quickly.

The neutral, self-loving and internal witness might say this about your fear: "I haven't had a job interview in two weeks. I'm about to jump out of my skin and scared to death about how this could play out. Yes, it is hard to trust my life right now."

Inner acceptance of anger might sound like this: "I am so freakin angry. He killed himself! Really! Who does that to people!? You're damned right I'm miffed. I have a right to be."

Truth be told, if you've been packing feelings for a long time, allowing yourself to begin to experience those feelings will not be easy. But allowing those feelings, hard as it may be, will eventually make your life more comfortable.

Step 3. Act

As you begin to experience the power of this going-through process by acknowledging and accepting all that you feel, you begin to naturally do things differently.

Steve was diagnosed with non-Hodgkin's lymphoma a year ago. Early going was tough, but recent good news about the illness has him feeling more optimistic. Even though he's feeling optimistic about his illness and despite support from his family and friends, Steve feels limited by a feeling he is unable to name.

What he feels and why is unclear, but by acknowledging the uncomfortableness, something happens. His senses sharpen about this particular uncomfortableness.

With this keener awareness, Steve realizes that the uncomfortable feeling is most pointed near the end of the day. While he doesn't like the feeling, he *accepts* it. By just accepting the feeling, Steve becomes more available to what the feeling might mean. So he explores what may be different about the end of the day. Hmmm, the phone doesn't ring as much, the kids are in bed and he and his wife have time alone.

Then the understanding gets even clearer. When Steve goes to bed early, he doesn't feel so uncomfortable. But when he stays up a while with his wife and watches TV, his uncomfortableness builds. So now he recognizes that when he's alone with his wife he feels the most uncomfortable. But that seems odd, because he loves her very much. He continues to pay attention to his inner life and this odd uncomfortableness.

When Steve is with his wife throughout the day, he notices that sometimes the uncomfortableness that he noticed at the end of the day appears as flashes. One morning his wife walks by while he's eating breakfast and says, "When's your next check-up, Honey? It's so hard not knowing what's going on with your lymphoma between these doctor visits." Instantly Steve recognizes just how uncomfortable her comment makes him. Then the dominos begin to fall.

He remembers many similar comments made by his wife when treatment started. He thought her comments were supporting him. So often they were, especially in the beginning. But now he sees her comments as laden with her fear, and he's growing increasingly uncomfortable with that because his prognosis is very positive. Steve's uncomfortableness with her fear has gotten so significant that he finds it difficult to sit alone with her in the evenings.

Having acknowledged and accepted his own uncomfortableness, new awareness has surfaced. How to resolve the situation now seems obvious. So Steve sits with his wife, whom he loves and misses, and shares openly how he may be pulling away because of the fear she expresses. Yes, there is some uncomfortableness even in the conversation, but she wants to hear him. Eventually, she agrees to work on communicating with less fear. She becomes aware that she is still frightened about his illness and decides to see a therapist. Before long, the fear and uncomfortableness in their relationship lessens and is eventually replaced with more contact and enjoyment. Steve's life feels better. So does his wife's.

If Steve had not first walked through and cleared his own emotions by acknowledging and accepting them, a new direction would have been less likely. Steve became more aware.

Change without awareness is like running blindfolded. When the blindfold created by unaddressed emotion comes off and you know better the layout of your inner landscape, movement in new direction happens with confidence, not because you have to or should but because you can now see a way.

CHAPTER SEVEN

Detours: Matters that Move You Off Your Recovery Road

Y ou've been driving a while. And like any long drive, there may be detours. A detour is anything that takes you away from the direct path. The direct path for most on the journey beyond hardship is recovery—recovery of healthy mind, emotions, relationships, body or spirit. A detour is anything that commands your attention, time, or energy enough to impact the steadiness and strength of that recovery.

Detours of Family

For those on a hardship journey, detours come in many forms. Most common are family detours. If you're handling the pressures of a new job after fourteen months without work and your teenage son gets kicked out of school, that's a detour.

Other detours may not be so obvious. Let's say you've taken on a focused recovery from alcohol. Then a close cousin decides he's going to be your advocate, even though you didn't ask him to be.

His intentions are the best. Your cousin is doing all kinds of Internet research about different treatments. That was OK for a while, but now you find yourself spending time explaining to your cousin why you haven't responded to his numerous e-mails, texts and phone calls. This can be a detour and in these kinds of situations, you may need to draw a line and limit the unwanted guidance. That's a form of self care.

Karen began therapy deeply depressed six months after a miscarriage. The loss hit her much harder than she expected, and healing that pain was challenge enough. But her sister had also been trying to have a baby. Karen's miscarriage rocked her sister to the core. When Karen showed up for counseling, she spent as much time talking about her sister as he did herself.

"Every time I see my sister, she starts sobbing," Karen reported. "I hate doing it, but I'm finding ways to stay away from her. I have to heal myself, but that seems farther and farther away because every time I see my sister it's like the band aid gets ripped off,"

As Karen settled into her own emotional experience, there was room for learning ways to stay separate from her sister's reactions. But the fact remained that her sister's pain made Karen's recovery more difficult. That's a detour.

Another trying detour is a family member deciding he or she knows what's best for you. All the sudden, you're defending your actions to this person at every turn. Precious time and energy may be spent diverting well-intentioned pushiness.

Similarly, a loved one may decide that the counselor, insurance company, doctor or agency you've been working with doesn't measure up. Consequently, every appointment with the professional you trust is followed by an inquisition led by the well-meaning loved one. In the worst case, you may begin to doubt the credibility of that professional. Now the road you're traveling feels busted up and progress can be slowed.

Oddly enough, another detour may be a spouse who feels jealous of all the attention you're getting as a result of the trauma you're surviving. Your spouse may regularly walk away from conversations you're having with others who are checking in on you. Your spouse may be irritable when you get off the phone with someone who is concerned about you.

Finally, hardship survivors may appear fine but they may feel anything but fine. Consequently, others may expect the survivor to perform according to pre-trauma standards. It's a detour when someone important believes you're not pulling your weight or using the tragedy as an excuse not to do your part.

Other Detours

Changes in the makeup of your support system can create detours. There's no question that secondary trauma may occur when confidants and key supporters in your life move, retire, or die. These include nurses, psychiatrists, religious advisors, internists, social workers, and family pets. When everything else feels out of control, the constancy of such essential supporters can hold a person together. Not surprisingly, many hardship survivors feel safer with folks from this group of supporters than they do with their own families. The presence of these helpers is important and their absence can be a detour.

Having a job threatened in some way can be a detour. Insurance issues are often a detour. Too many people stopping by for too many visits can be a detour. Folks telling you stories of all their hardships may be a detour. Criticism for honest emotion or tears can be a detour. Lastly, relapse of an addiction or recurrence of an illness is more than a detour for most. It's a crash.

CHAPTER EIGHT

Rest Stop #2: One-Step Anxiety Management

Have you had the pleasure of traveling with a four-legged friend? Did you bring your dog on this particular trip? Not a bad idea, given all we know about pets and stress reduction. Did you ever notice what your dog does when it gets alarmed? Usually a dog will bark and then stand motionless without even breathing. We do the same thing. Watch. When something startles you, you freeze and stop breathing. At that moment, your whole system is receiving a message that says, "Warning! It's not safe. Don't relax. Don't trust. Be afraid. Be ready!" Oddly enough, it's a wonderful and primitive reaction that has preserved the species, because it initiates chemical changes in the body that make us more adept at managing physical threats. When you hold your breath after being startled, the body floods your arms and legs with oxygen, producing a level of alertness, readiness, and tension throughout.

People sometimes get startled during the journey of life. However, there's evidence that living in this alert state can be costly, particularly when it happens unconsciously, and the body holds the tension longer and longer. This prolonged startled experience becomes anxiety, and this state is especially troublesome for those who were anxious before tragedy changed their lives.

An ongoing, "It's not safe. Don't relax. Don't trust. Be afraid. Be ready!" feeling can be exhausting. Fortunately, there is a way to interrupt this uncomfortable state. It's based on physiology. At a primitive level, the alert response begins when you hold your breath. For that reason, the breath becomes central in interrupting anxiety. Using this key, here's a One-Step Anxiety Management technique:

STEP 1: Brrrrreeeeeaaaathe

Breathing has two parts: inhale and exhale. It's biology. When you stop breathing, you invite tension and fear. When you breathe fully, you invite relaxation and safety. Fear and trust are opposites, and the breath can be used to induce either. Short, rapid breaths or no breaths at all come with fear. Long, regular, full breaths come with trust. If you find yourself feeling anxious—experiencing those "don't relax, don't trust, be afraid, be ready" feelings—take deep breaths. The body is hard wired to shift gears when you breathe fully. Deep breaths will help chase away the anxiety.

As we will explore in later chapters, it can be useful to notice fear and work with it, rather than chase it away. But whenever you feel the need for a quick fix, changing your breathing can provide that. (By the way, it would be good to begin all the exercises in this book with conscious breathing.)

Now, if you're a two-step kind of person, here's one to go along with the brrreeeaaathe step. Suggest the following thoughts to yourself as you breathe: "It's OK. In this moment, everything is all right."

If you want, follow this up by being aware of your legs and feet. Notice as you deeply breathe how your feet feel against your socks or shoes. You might be surprised at the quick and pleasant results of this simple activity. Combined, these tips provide a fast way to feel a bit more comfortable on your journey, especially if you're anxious.*

*If you suffer from serious, persistent anxiety, professional help and/or medical intervention may be necessary.

CHAPTER NINE

Travel Tips for Couples

I n previous chapters, we've spoken about relationship changes, personal pressures, and detours. Consider these tips when traveling with someone on the journey beyond hardship to circumvent together as many of those slow downs and detours as possible.

Travel Tips for Partners of Hardship Survivors

- As a survivor once said, "If you don't got it, you don't get it." In other words, if you haven't experienced the survivor's trauma, you really can't understand it. Consequently, saying you do usually doesn't help. Just be with the survivor when he or she needs you.

- Keep in mind that life demands, pain, fatigue, and endless logistics can affect everyone's mood. The survivor is not his or her usual self mentally, physically, emotionally or relationally. It's best not to expect your partner to be the same as before. This expectation leads to frustration for everybody.

- Survivors making their way through tragedy experience kindness like medicine and unkindness like salt in wounds.

- D.A.A.A. = <u>D</u>on't <u>A</u>ssume <u>A</u>nything—<u>A</u>sk. Don't assume the survivor needs to be cheered on. Don't assume he or she doesn't. Don't assume the survivor needs to feel hopeful today. Don't assume he or she doesn't. Don't assume the survivor needs to eat more, exercise more, sleep more, or have more sex. Don't assume he or she doesn't. Don't assume the survivor needs your company or conversation. Don't assume he or she doesn't. Instead of assuming, ask the simple question, "What can I do for you right now that would be most helpful?" And remember, what is needed right now could change in a minute.

- Did you know when you tell everyone you see that the survivor "handles this so well," or "always has a great sense of humor, even with the pain," or "never complains," you may actually be sending the message to that survivor, "Stay strong." So where is the survivor supposed to go with the tough feelings that naturally occur? Are you willing to be strong for the survivor?

- Repeatedly telling someone who is hurting, "You look great," may discount that person's pain. On the other hand, when people in pain (physical or emotional) are simply listened to, their pain often decreases, and tough emotions dissipate more quickly.

- Support people, you may not have suffered the survivor's trauma, but you have rights in all this, too. Yes, you're going to give the survivor more leeway, but don't give yourself away in the process. Don't let yourself be taken advantage of. That's not good for anybody. In taking care of yourself, it's OK to say things like, "Look, I know you're exhausted and frustrated, but talk to me with respect," or, "You need time alone once in a while, and so do I."

• A time may come when you just want to put all this behind you. As a result, you may start acting like nothing ever happened. For the short run, that attitude may get you through. Such an approach does seem to work for some folks over the long haul. But the mental, emotional, physical, and relational ramifications of what has happened are significant, and not just for the survivor. For you, too. Never allowing yourself to process any of the ramifications may take a toll.

• The person surviving the hardship is busy taking care of himself/herself. You're responsible for you. It's very important that you maintain your own health and well-being. Mounting evidence shows that when someone you love is traumatized, you as the support person may suffer psychological distress much like that of the person suffering the hardship.[9] Additionally, chronic illness in a partner may also negatively affect the support person's physical and mental health.[10]

Travel Tips For Hardship Survivors

- The person supporting you loves you. He or she wants so much to take your pain away—wants so much to help. But in many cases, your primary support person doesn't know first hand what you're going through. As a result, he or she may not understand. Don't expect that.

  The person supporting you is also not a mind reader. Don't expect that either. When you simply tell your support person what you need, you help him or her avoid making assumptions, and you're more likely to get what's important to you.

- Your support person may find it difficult to leave you alone or do things that are good for him or herself. However, if that person doesn't respect his or her own needs, you will both live in the resentment that builds. If you're currently homebound, earnestly encourage your support person to take time for him or herself. Invite someone else to stay with you if you need that. You have to be loving but firm about this if you really want your support person to stay well. You'll both benefit from it.

- As the survivor, it's possible that you feel powerless. You may feel as if you have very little control of your situation or emotions. Consequently, you may be looking for something or someone to control as a way to make yourself feel better— as a way to feel some sense of mastery in this difficult circumstance. Many times the person you try to control most is the person closest to you. This can look like nitpicking; like nothing that person does is right. Remember, you are not the only one with needs.

- A time may come when you want to put all this behind you. As a result, you may start to act as if nothing ever happened. For the short run, that attitude may get you through. And such an approach does seem to work for some folks over the long haul. But something did happen. The mental, emotional, physical, and relational ramifications of that "something" can be significant. Never allowing yourself to visit any of those affected aspects of yourself may take a toll.

- Finally, your courage and heroism may uplift many people. That can be wonderful. But if you never say no as the survivor, take a break, or let others know what you need in a direct way, resentment can build in you. Your support person will likely become the target of that anger. Always saying yes and rarely saying no may be a way of life for you, which makes that pattern difficult to undo. Anger is the focus of Chapter 20, which also offers special sections on learning to say no.

Travel Tips For Both Hardship Survivors and Their Partners

Accept one another where you are, not where you think the other should be. Out of your own need, you may give love only when the person you're on the journey with hits the mark you have deemed as gold standard: "There's that great smile." This statement sends the message, "If you, my love, are not happy on the outside all the time, you're letting me down." This can burden the heart.

Next, be mindful of who and how many you tell about the tragedy. If one of you doesn't want the whole world to know, the other is wise to support that. Yes, a community of caring people who know about your situation can and often does make the journey easier for both the survivor and the partner. However, folks can do funny things with the news of your hardship. They can one-up you—tell stories of someone who had the same tragedy but add, "They lost everything," or "Hers was much worse."

These stories and the emotion that comes with them can drain you. Not only that, there's often a point of diminishing return related to the number of people you share your experience with. If everywhere you go people ask about what happened, you might feel trapped—no place to be free of it. Many survivors have told me that they just want to be treated normally. This isn't denial. There are times people dealing with tragedy just don't want to go there. It is nice to have some surroundings that are tragedy-free. When you're there, even for a little bit, the hardship isn't—like maybe at a book club or gym. That can be a relief.

Sex and Hardship

Some men and women surviving hardship barely skip a beat in their typical sexual relations. These people can satisfy and be satisfied by their mates. For a lot of other people, navigating a sex life after hardship isn't that simple.

For many in the beginning of the journey beyond hardship, sex is low on the priority list. Too many matters and emotions require managing. In time, however, the physically intimate part of relationship gains strength as a need. Often the need of one lover is not matched by the need of the other. Strong couples manage this well. Yet, a life trauma can wreak havoc on even the surest relationships. Someone has to take the initiative in bringing to light what may be hiding beneath the surface.

When highly stressed, both men and women can find orgasm difficult to achieve. Spouses often feel inadequate if they aren't able to satisfy or be satisfied by their mates. This can feed any depression that may be present, which itself can weaken libido. This experience can put a dent in self-esteem. This lowered esteem may circle back to limited sex drive, sexual functioning, or satisfaction.

Women and men whose tragedy leaves them with scars may be especially sensitive to being seen unclothed. This can be disarming to their mates. Mates may feel unwanted themselves, or confused, struggling to understand what would be most helpful. More than one survivor has talked about undressing only in closets or behind closed doors. You usually can't go wrong by gently and lovingly opening this issue for pillow talk, wrapped in lots of acceptance.

Lovers also get confused by when, what, and how to touch. There can be uncertainty about whether the lack of interest in sex is a product of the situation or a reflection of the relationship. When one partner initiates, the other may act as if the distance of recent history is still in play. Is this a sign that my lover wants to get closer, or is it going to pass? Does my mate want more contact or more time? Is this a hug thing, or something more?

Patience with each other at times like this will help a lot. All these questions are great topics of discussion. Don't wait until you find yourself in a situation of sexual uncertainty. Talk about it over dinner or sometime before you lie down. Remember not to assume anything. It's a good way to prevent hurt feelings.

Hardship survivors or their partners may experience the need to be the dutiful spouse in the bedroom, which is being sexual because he or she needs that, even when you're not interested. Of course, most couples have varying degrees of desire at any given time, and it's not uncommon for one partner to be more interested than the other. This kind of compromise has its place. But physical intimacy impacts us in profound psychological ways. As a result, patterns of this sort of sexual compromise can do damage. Be careful of routinely suppressing your own feelings. Honesty and realness build trust. Trust supports a more satisfying sex life. Dutifulness then becomes moot.

If you want to be heard, listen. People often don't hear until they've been heard. Hearing your partner communicates respect. When any of us feels respected, we relax, and feel more open. That leads to feeling more loved and loving. That creates an atmosphere where a sex life can flourish.

CHAPTER TEN

Rest Stop #3: Stress Bustin'

Stress is an Inside Job

W hether you're traveling with someone or alone, most trips usually have their stressful moments. This is especially true with the journey beyond hardship. Some basic stress management information might be helpful as you travel.

First, let's distinguish *stress* from *stressor*. Imagine that a hail storm blows through your neighborhood and a dozen people on your block have cars parked on the street. All twelve cars are damaged. In this case, hail is the *stressor*, the external event. However, your neighbors could have twelve different levels of *stress* based on each person's reaction. In other words, most stressors happen outside us; stress happens inside us.

There will always be *stressors*. But how much *stress* you experience is based on how you respond to those events. Believe it or not, how much stress you feel is a choice. Consider the power that gives you for the quality of your life.

Recognizing Stress

If you're dealing with a hardship in your life, you probably feel stressed. That's expected. But it is possible to recognize just how stressed you're getting. This recognition positions you perfectly to regulate the intensity of your stress, as well as regulate how long you stay in that stress.

In other words, when the stressors related to your tragedy affect you, you can learn to recognize your reaction, be it anger, fear, sadness: "OK, no question I'm getting worked up." This is quite different from just reacting. With that simple internal response, you give yourself a tad bit of distance from the situation.

How? Because it's impossible to be 100% immersed in a reaction, and simultaneously notice that you're having it. When you notice your reaction, some part of you is actually not having that reaction. It's too busy noticing the reaction. The part that notices is beginning to teach you to Read The Edges.

Stress and Choice

By noticing your stress level, you can create. You can make a choice. You are creating what the next moment of your life will feel like: "Do I really want to get this worked up?"

First of all, you may be thinking, "There's no way I'm able to make a choice about how angry I get when I find out insurance isn't covering heavier plywood required to replace my roof ripped off by the tornado."

Many people have had a similar response to this notice notion. Yet, many of those same people are now more comfortable, even with the stressor of their difficult situation, because they are making choices about how they respond to their lives.

Again, we each get to choose what our next moment is going to feel like. The more you practice seeing yourself reacting to stressors, the more sense it makes that you are choosing how your next moment will feel. Who doesn't want to feel better? The best news of all is that when you notice, you call back your power as you choose— the power to make the kind of life you want, regardless of what's happening outside you. Regardless of the stressors.

Most great religions speak clearly about free will. That's the truth—we all get to choose. Every moment we are choosing how we respond to the world around us. Every moment. By these constant and multitudinous choices, we create the quality of our lives. We just don't usually think of choosing our feelings or thoughts. But our thoughts and feelings are the only things we truly have absolute choice in. When we understand this and start making conscious choices, rather than just reacting to all that's happening around us, we start creating our lives. This is tremendously exciting and it's how we get back the power that is our birth right.

What You Have vs. What You Want

The stress you feel from the stressor of your hardship is the stress of wanting something you're not getting: you want peace, you want health, you want security.

Stress (the inner experience of emotional discomfort) then equals something (your life trauma) blocking you from what you want {peace, joy, health, prosperity}.

Stress Bustin' is really about Choice. And it's not so much about what you choose but that you choose.

Are you aware of how many choices you've made in the last twenty four hours, starting with what time you got up? You might say, "I guess I chose what time to get up, but if I didn't get up, I'd be late for work." OK, so you chose to get up to be on time. Then you might say, "I have to be on time, or I'll lose my job." OK, so you've chosen to keep your job.

The idea is, when we live aware of our choices, our life comes alive. We start to see it as self-created rather than imposed. Yow. When you press this, you realize that everything you have is what you want.

Wait. Hear me out, if you can. Think about it. If what you have isn't what you want, why don't you have something else? Consider that for just a second. (We'll talk about *having* tragedy and *having* pain in a minute.)

I shared the concept that "We have what we want or we'd have something else" with an audience one afternoon. A woman in the crowd who had been restless in her chair for a while finally stood up and proclaimed, "My husband left me with three kids. The youngest is this big. Do you think this is what I want?!"

I said, "You know, I read last winter about a woman who left her baby in a gym bag in the dead of winter in a city park. You could do that."

She snapped, "I've been sitting here thinking you were crazy. Now I know you are. I would never do that!"

"Exactly," I said. "You would never do that because what you want is to love and value your children so they will feel loved and valued in life. You are choosing to stay for that reason, hard as it may be." Nobody was making her raise those kids. As long as she was willing to deal with the consequences, she too could walk. She really could. What she had was a choice, and through the discussion she began to see what she was choosing. When she understood this notion, she changed. Her body language shifted. She tasted a tinge of her freedom then—the freedom that can fill us when we recognize our choosing.

A guy came up to me after a presentation to national store managers. Briefcase in hand he said, "Greg, that stuff about stress bustin' is all fine and dandy, but you know what would really take care of my stress? A johnboat, a six-pack, and the Florida Keys. I live in a stinkin' town, with a mortgage as big as my neighborhood and a truckload of kids. The only thing that's gonna touch my stress is The Keys."

"So why don't you go upstairs, make a few calls, and go?" I asked. He looked at me like I was nuts. "Yeah," I said, "Call your family, pack up the works, and go. Who's stoppin' you? Now, you may be out there fishing one day, and some guys paddle up in suits saying, 'Hi, we're from Visa,' but if you're willing to deal with that, go!"

He looked at me for a second, then cocked his head like a pup. He got it. Nobody was making him live in a stinking town. Nobody was making him stay in his job or his house, or his marriage for that matter. When he got the power of his past, present, and future choices, something lifted from him. He understood that what he had was what he must want, or he'd have something else. The same is true for each of us.

"What about this cancer?" "What about my house being torn in half by the hurricane?" "What about my child dying?" These are, of course, external circumstances over which we have no control. We, in our human selves, would never choose disaster or disease for ourselves or anyone we love.

Yet, even within these, there are choices. I kept a little sign on my bulletin board for years that read: "Sometimes all we have control of is where we place our attention." Naturally, if you've just gotten news of a diagnosis or divorce or job cut, it's normal to feel very scared, or angry, or hurt. But in these moments, too, it is possible to become choiceful rather than reactive. Once, a client talked about seeing a call coming in on her smart phone. She knew by the number displayed that the call was not going to be easy: "So I held my phone in my hand, and said to myself, 'How do I wanna react?'" The client was making a choice about how and where to place her attention.

Another question you may ask is, "What about choice and physical discomfort?" Well, there's a Harvard professor by the name of Shinzen Young who has had tremendous success helping people reduce their levels of physical pain through mental exercises that shift attention. See the bibliography at the end of this book for information about his work.

Fundamentally, the simple act of recognizing choice makes a lot of rough circumstances feel better. The freedom comes in two ways:

first, knowing you have, do, and will choose (at least internally) in almost every situation; secondly, deciding to choose things that make you feel better, not worse. Your life is not imposed. Situations or events may be. How you respond is usually not.

The Three-Step Stress Bustin' Process

Step 1. Identify What You Want

Perhaps you feel stressed during the holidays because they remind you of a painful time—someone's death or the anniversary of your divorce. These difficult holiday reminders happen a lot. Let's assume you've been on the hardship journey a while now, and most of the time you feel better. But the holidays still get to you. The tough feelings that come with facing another holiday is your stress. In knowing what your stress is, what you usually want is the opposite of that stress. In this case then, what you want is joy or peace this birthday or holiday.

Step 2. Ask Yourself, "Is This Worth Having?"

Step 2 is about evaluating whether or not what you want is really worth having. Go back to wanting more peace this holiday. It seems pretty obvious. In answer to the Step 2 question, "Is this worth having?" how could peace not be worth having? Well, here's one way. What if your spouse had a persistent pain in the lower abdomen? And what if that spouse decided on peace of mind, in spite of the pain? Some people are able to achieve great peace in the face of pain through mental exercise. But what if the pain and the lack of peace were messages from your spouse's body to take action? In this case, paying attention to the pain and seeing a doctor would be useful. Therefore, ignoring the pain as a means to peace may not be worth it.

What if you're stressed during the holidays because your teenage daughter refuses to tell you how she feels when it comes to the family's hardship? The stress is your ongoing concern that she is holding everything in. What you want is for her to express herself to you. What's the block here? Could the block be your expectation that she talk with you about what's happened to the family? Maybe she's sharing her feelings with her friends as a way of protecting you.

Is her expressing herself to you worth having? Maybe it is. Maybe it isn't. That's for you to decide.

Step 3. Choose

Once you're clear about what you want and have decided it really is worth having, Step 3 is to make choices to get what you want. Let's say you decide, yes more peace and joy this birthday or holiday is worthwhile. Having made that decision, what will you choose to bring more peace and joy? Learn some anxiety management techniques? But what if you've decided that learning anxiety management techniques right now will eat up what precious little energy you have? So be it. Maybe you'll choose instead to just wrap that fear up with a bow, and put it out of your mind until after the holiday. Not because you just want to ignore it, but because you've decided leaving it alone right now is best. All right. You get to choose.

That's the power of Stress Bustin'—living fully conscious of your ability to choose, every minute, every day. The actions you choose are important. The awareness that you do choose is life-giving. You are not powerless about the stress. Maybe powerless about the stressor, but not the stress.

Say you decide that it is important for you and your daughter to talk. You have been watching her, and she seems depressed: grades are slipping, she spends a lot of time alone, she doesn't seem like herself. So, what will you choose to do about that? Maybe you'll start with a phone call to the school counselor, or speak at length about it with your spouse to figure out how to respond as parents. Good. Or maybe you'll decide it's actually better for everybody to simply keep a close eye on her, but not say anything right now. You know her best. That's fine. So when your daughter continues to hide her feelings, you recognize that, but instead of getting stressed, you remember the choice you have made to just pay attention.

While acting so precisely on these kinds of decisions isn't as simple as one, two, three, the more you practice the power of choice, the more fluid it all becomes. The intent is not to figure out what is the right or wrong thing to do. It's about choice. It's about living fully aware that so much of your life (even if it's only your inner life) is a product of your choices. A life of choice is much different from an emotional, mental, or even spiritual life that feels imposed by someone or something else. Living aware of choice lowers stress. Life gets better.

CHAPTER ELEVEN

Mountaintops: Seeing Life from a New Perspective

D o you know what it's like to drive through a beautiful landscape, climb to elevated terrain, and look down? The view from these higher heights is different and often better. Hardship has the potential to do the same to your life perspective, though this is difficult to imagine in the early going.

Hundreds of hardship survivors as well as personal and professional hardship support people have reported that life was not the same once they journeyed beyond. Life after the trauma had more meaning. Simple things mattered more. Some say they began to take better care of themselves. They learned to say no. Some said small concerns bothered them less. Some found their voices and speak up more often. Many found peace and improved marriages.

Many explain how their values have shifted since making it through a tough time: "There's more to life than work," or, "I'm tired of being scared about everything." Others experience more compassion for all who suffer. In still others, something inside pops open and joy comes out.

Some discover for the first time who they are. Tragedy has a way of trimming off all that is not real so only the truth remains. Sometimes, folks on the journey beyond hardship change in ways their mates can't or won't. Some let another's love in for the first time. What proceeds from this love is a deep and powerful care for humankind.

For others on the journey great pools of hurt, sadness, or anger are uncovered. Fortified by the strength required to overcome their trauma, these people dive into those turbulent waters, swimming for the solid shore of greater wholeness. And from those waters a new person is born. Like natural birth: first there's discomfort, then pain, then great pain, then birth, new life and real joy.

From the high ground of survival life may look very different. It's curious when the self changes like this. Even your God can seem different. Going through hardship and tragedy is some of the deepest work for a soul. Serious life struggles appear to open a window somewhere in the spirit of a person. Some climb through to a new land. Others don't. There is meaning in each way.

There's a second aspect of climbing to higher heights. Once safely on the other side of hardship, some climb to an emotional survivor's high. The line between a richly improved life and an unhealthy emotional high is sometimes pretty thin.

Surely you've met those whose confidence seems hollow with survivor high. In their fervor, they may find it difficult to tolerate any experience or worldview different from the one they now clutch.

Consequently, distance can be created between them and those who really love them—those who can help them climb down safely. Their joy is fragile. Their focus is narrow. Intoxication with the newfound self might only be another anesthesia against the old pain still unplowed deep in their bellies.

When I walked into the group therapy room, I saw Connie for the first time. She had an unsteady smile. Most new group members do. But hers was different. It held more than the usual discomfort that comes with meeting new people under the circumstances of trauma or (in this case) illness. I was immediately aware that her voice was carrying over most of the other group members as they chatted before we got started. It was hard not to notice the force behind Connie's words. Entering the group room, I caught pieces of what she was saying: "…and if you don't completely believe you're going to get better, you won't."

The custom with new members of these weekly groups is to let long-term members introduce themselves first. This helps take the pressure off new members, as they watch the others. We also make sure that, as the last one to introduce him or herself, the new member can take as much time as needed on this first day.

Connie seemed uneasy as she listened. Seasoned group members, along with their introductions, often update the group on their weeks. This includes comments like, "I also found out I have to get additional testing done, and I'm pretty scared. I'd like to talk about this more after intros."

The closer it got to Connie's turn, the more uncomfortable she seemed, squirming on the edge of her seat and looking at her watch, purse still in hand. "This just doesn't have a good feeling to me. . . . Oh, my name is Connie," was her introduction. "I had bladder cancer. I was diagnosed six weeks ago," she blurted. "I don't have it anymore. Surgery got rid of it, and I am doing all I can to stay well," beginning to shake as the words fell out.

"I'm afraid you're all very negative," Connie shuddered. "I heard people talking about being sad. And someone said they were afraid. I'm not. I am going to beat this. . . . I mean I have beaten this," she restated. She wrestled with the tears coming to her eyes but couldn't allow them as she said, "We can all beat this, but you have to be more hopeful. I'll stay and see how I feel, but this group may not be for me."

Group members were reacting to Connie. Some of the new people were picking up her angst and beginning to squirm, too. The more mature group members simply sat with openness, both to Connie and their own feelings and reactions. As for those members who weren't quite sure how to react, they looked to me. Veteran members knew it was tough starting in the group, so an experienced member spoke up: "Connie, being new to a group like this can be pretty uncomfortable. What would be most helpful to you right now?"

"I don't know. Can somebody say something good?" she responded.

"I remember my first day with the group," offered another group member. "I was the only one with lung cancer and wondered if I would connect to anyone else."

A male group member spoke up: "Yeah, I had a hard time with all this emotional stuff, but now I wouldn't miss the group for anything."

At that, Connie jumped up and shot to the door saying, "I can't do this. God bless you all. I love you. Please be happy." That was the last time we saw Connie. She did exactly what she needed to do. However, I felt sure the powerful pain just below the surface for Connie would soon break through, and she wouldn't have a group to support her when it did.

Chapter Twelve

Rest Stop #4: Values and Voting with Your Feet

The exercise in this chapter helps you gain awareness of how you vote—how your values are represented by your actions rather than by your words. Let the exercise inform you. It's for your eyes only. Be genuine with your responses and you'll get more out of it. If you find that what you say about your values matches your actions, then you probably have, more or less, what you want in your life. If you find that what you say about your values does not match your actions, you will then know which actions to take to make your life feel better. Taking these actions, freely and by choice, will make you feel more like you have what you want in your life.

There are no right or wrong responses to this exercise. It's just information. Let the information speak to you in its own way. There are no score comparisons. Just the chance to increase your awareness.

Values and Voting with Your Feet

Step 1. Take Some Time. Make a List of the Ten Things You Value Most

Give yourself whatever time you need. Try to zero in on the top ten most important features, actions, people, practices, beliefs, etc., in your life today. This can be anything: your family, your faith, your exercise plan, your financial plan, your time, your car, your breakfast, your doctor, your dog, your job, your diary, beauty, serenity, anything.

Step 2. Prioritize Your List

When you're ready, list the ten items you came up with in rank order down the left side of a sheet of paper with the most important item from your list at the top and the least important item at the bottom. Feel free to use the form at the end of this chapter.

Step 3. Make Five Columns Across the Top of Your Page With the Following Headings:

How Often   How Long   How Much   Feeling   Give Up

To create the columns, draw five lines about an inch apart down your sheet, to the right of the prioritized list of your ten most important items. Here are the meanings of each column heading:

<u>How Often</u>: How regularly do you engage in this feature? Put the number 10 in this column beside the feature from your original

top-ten list that you do the most often. Put the number 1 in this column beside the feature from your list that you do the least often. If you listed beauty, for example, on your original list, how often do you find it, or how often do you create experiences that expose you to beauty? If, in this way, you experience beauty more often than you do any other thing from your list, then put the number 10 beside "Beauty" under the column, "How Often." If you put basketball on your list, and you play a lot, but not as often as you experience beauty, then you would put the number 9 beside basketball.

How Long: When you do engage in this feature, how much time do you spend? Put the number 10 in this column beside the feature from your list of ten that you spend the most time with. Put the number 1 in this column beside the feature from your list that you spend the least time with.

How Much: When you do engage in this feature, how much does it cost? Prioritize your list in the same way you did under the first two headings, i.e., 10 beside the item that you spend the most money on, etc.

Feeling: When you do engage in this feature, how good does it make you feel? Put the number 10 in this column beside the feature from your list of ten that makes you feel the best, etc.

Give Up: Which of the ten features from your list would you most willingly give up? Put the number 1 in this column beside the feature from your list that you would be most willing to give up completely.

Put the number 10 in this column beside the feature from your list that you would be least willing to give up completely.

Finally, total all the numbers to the right of each of your original ten important items. So, do you vote with your feet? If this column of totals is highest at the top, decreases as it goes down the page, and is lowest at the bottom, then you do vote with your feet. If it doesn't, then your actions suggest those things that are truly most important to you have the higher totals to the right, and those things that are least important to you have the lower totals to the right.

If you find there's an activity or belief or even person you spend a lot of money, a lot of time or a lot of energy on, but that didn't make your list, decide what's true for you regarding that activity, belief or person. Decide whether or not you want to continue spending.

What matters about this exercise is that it offers you a chance to discover more of what you really value. The purpose is simply to invite you to pay more attention to the people, places, experiences, and beliefs that bring you life.

Vote With Your Feet						
YOUR TOP-TEN ITEMS BELOW	How Often?	How Long?	How Much?	Feeling?	Give Up?	Total Points
1.						
2.						
3.						
4.						
5.						
6.						
7.						
8.						
9.						
10.						

CHAPTER THIRTEEN

Who's Really Driving? View from the Support Person's Window

E verybody on the healing journey needs refreshments, regardless of who's driving, because anyone closely involved with a hardship survivor can be deeply affected by that survivor's journey. This chapter is for those taking the journey *with* the survivor.

Susan's best buddy, her father, was battling his traumatic situation full force. Because she was moving to be near him, Susan came to group therapy for the last time.

"My dad's fighting with all his might," she spoke through her tears. "He's throwing punches, and taking punches, bleeding, and down on one knee. And all I can do is stand in the corner and hold the towel." That's a powerful description of what it's like to be central in the life of someone surviving hardship. It aptly represents the sense of utter helplessness shared by so many support people. Given the gravity of the survivor's circumstance, this weight carried by loved ones often goes unnoticed.

Being a Support: Newly Defined Roles

For support people, this weight is felt day to day, if not moment to moment. Now the support person is not only responsible for groceries, laundry, kids, and the lawn, but add to that finances, special appointments, and the extended family. And be sure to include the new roles of counselor and provider just to name a few.

Behind the scenes, the support person may be running interference with family members of the hardship survivor. Support people may also have discreet discussions with the survivor's employer. The fine line between supporting the survivor and the survivor's need for self-governance can be tricky. Through all this the survivor may still feel they're behind the wheel. But it's the support person that often carries the bulk of the load, and often feels like the one doing the driving.

Jim's father, Allen, was a retired widower that insisted on working part-time at a hardware store, even though his Alzheimer's was worsening. Allen would tell Jim of problems at work. In time, Jim made a call to his dad's boss to fill her in on Allen's condition. Allen also used credit cards to buy expensive tools he was no longer capable of using. As Allen's executor, Jim discretely began to take control of his father's finances. Jim was gently taking the wheel.

Support people don't know how much to push and how much to be patient. I've heard many survivors say if it wasn't for their loved one giving them a solid nudge once in a while, they wouldn't have made it. Yet many survivors wish people would just back off. For many support people, trying to find this "nudge them—give them space," balance takes a toll.

The Support Person's Experience

Support people become tired, but they are not likely to acknowledge it. Support people often don't receive support and often don't know to ask for it. Support people often feel invisible. While tragedy survivors may be asked, "How are you?" the support person's painful experience may go unrecognized.

While it's essential for support people to take care of themselves, they often feel lost in the endless to-do list, meetings, moods, and care requirements. Support people forget who they really are. They have morphed so many times to the situation at hand that they don't feel anchored in a personality. What often comes before this loss of self is the use of historically effective crisis responses. But then those tried and true responses stop working: "Who should I be now? What should I do?"

Support people may think ESP is critical for getting the job done, but they don't have it. They can't read the survivor's mind. Support people believe they have just found the right thing to say, the right food to prepare, or the right way to hold the survivor and just like that, the survivor's want changes. All this worsens the support person's nagging sense of helplessness.

Sometimes nothing seems to be working. This can eventually lead to a surrender in the support person: "I don't know what to do anymore. I guess I just have to take it day to day." Such letting go can be powerfully good. It can be a way to growth. However, it can also be powerfully tormenting and confusing.

Support people may doubt the strength of the survivor's love for them and their love for the survivor. Most work this out, but some couples don't. Hardship could be the most intense pressure endured in their relationship.

Many loved ones wish they had taken the hardship hit. On the other hand, support people sometimes wish it could all just be over. In especially painful and prolonged hardship recoveries, support people can catch themselves wishing the survivor's emotional, mental, or physical pain would end.

Because it hurts so much to see someone you love pressed in pain, you may wish death would release them. If the support person is thinking these thoughts, the survivor probably is, too. In strong relationships, even such tough thoughts are brought to light, and the darkness felt by both the support person and the survivor lifts a bit.

Avoiding Resentment

Support people forget to send the bill, turn off the stove, take the kids, or fix the door. But remembering is on their must-do list. Loved ones usually expect themselves to be strong, to hold the survivor up. It is part of our culture to focus away from ourselves when someone we love is in real need. Thank goodness for this instinct. It works wonderfully, except when it doesn't.

Support people and survivors both know this point when selflessness stops working. This breaking point usually comes long after the tragic event. It may show up when the survivor (in the loved one's opinion) is having a hard time moving on with his or her life. We are talking about the point when everybody's nerves are cooked. The support person can't hold back his or her feelings another minute, and can't wait on the survivor one more time. However, this point is often not reckoned with.

One way to avoid reaching this breaking point is for the support person to begin to acknowledge, accept, and act on his or her own needs, not just the needs of the survivor. Actually, the sooner the support person is able to do this respectfully, the better.

I was discussing this point during a TV interview when the host said, "But Greg, don't you think the survivor is saying, 'Look, I'm the one that's really hurting here. I have a right to be taken care of, no matter what. For better or for worse, in sickness and in health.'" I said, "Yep, and the support person has a right to have boundaries."

It's not an either/or. It's one of those "boths." If the support person doesn't take care of him or herself, tremendous resentment will build. If you, as a support person, feel resentment, take a good look at how well a job you're doing taking care of yourself. First of all, there's a good chance your resentment will lessen when you mobilize your own needs. Do something about them.

Secondly, if you really want to do the best for the one you're caring for, take care of yourself. Don't think for a second that your resentment is not experienced in every tone, touch, word, and gesture you offer. Equally important is the fact that your resentment will infect the quality of your life, too. This makes for a long and difficult journey.

Several survivors who have become support people have shared that it was easier being the survivor. How so? Survivors who become support people cite the tremendous helplessness of their new role. For example, the survivor knows just how much pain he or she is in, but the support person is left to speculate, never really knowing.

Whether or not it's easier to be a survivor or a support person is subjective. But science shows that the increased burden experienced by someone taking care of an ill loved one, for example, was significantly correlated to worsening health for that support person. Over 50 percent of the support people in one study showed measurable signs of depression.[11]

Support people, no matter what the hardship, it's crucial that you take care of yourselves.

CHAPTER FOURTEEN

Rest Stop #5: Clearing the Clouds of Trauma and Anxiety

A long the hardship journey, survivors and support people alike often find anxiety an unwelcomed companion. In a previous chapter, we spoke about the natural startle response and its impact on the body's chemistry. Anxiety can create the same physical changes. The difference, however, is that while the startle response is usually triggered by an external event, anxiety may be induced by a seed thought or an image from inside you. This scary, initial seed thought generates a second fearful thought, then another…and you're off to the races. The mind starts whirling.

Eventually, the nervous system reacts to this internally generated feeling of fear as it does the external startle, cutting oxygen to the brain. Thinking then becomes difficult. The brain is lacking the fuel it needs to do its job. Soon, there is nothing but feelings—dark, scary feelings.

As one survivor put it, "It's not fear I feel. It's terror." Whatever name we give, anxiety is one of the most frequently experienced emotions on the journey beyond. And yet as common as it is, most have learned to avoid anxiety or push it away. Oddly enough, anxiety by its nature seems to intensify when we push against it. The following exercise is designed to relieve the pressure of anxiety and the frightful images that often come with it, by entering right into it, rather than avoiding it:

Clearing the Clouds of Trauma and Anxiety

Step 1. See Your Experience as a Distant Cloud

Recurring traumatic images or anxiety cloud your mind. They make thoughts jagged and unclear and difficult. Concentration becomes less and less possible. Before long, fear dominates you.

Frank Herbert in his book *Dune* shares some valuable notions about anxiety. His basic message is that you are not your fear. You may see its coming and its going, but you are not your fear.[12] This exercise is offered to help you put this profound concept into action.

To see your experience as a distant cloud, try this simple visualization. First of all, imagine you're in a theater sitting away from the stage. Next, imagine the traumatic incident you keep flashing back to taking place on the stage, far away from you. Or if you're anxious, visualize yourself being anxious up there on the stage. Just watch this scene for a moment as best you can without emotion, as if it belonged to someone else—like a scene from a play.

It's most important to notice your experience in this distant way. Stay with this part of Step 1 until you have the sense that your experience is up there on the stage. Be patient and try not to wrestle with the visualization. Once your mind's eye sees your experience as up there on the stage, imagine that all the feelings associated with this event gently rise up above the scene in the form of a cloud that is still out there.

For example, maybe you're family was in a car accident and your youngest was injured. And whenever you're not busy your mind serves up images of that horror, along with paralyzing fear.

If you can, allow yourself to watch that terrible episode happening up on the stage. Your brain is already viewing the event, but in a chaotic, uncontrolled way. By seeing it occurring on the stage, you're halfway there. By placing the uncontrolled scene on the stage, you actually initiate some internal control.

If it's too much to see the accident occurring on the stage, that's OK. Don't push it. Instead, consider seeing yourself on the stage in this moment with the fright you feel about the event.

Next, see the tremendous fear associated with the accident rising up from the stage like smoke and forming a cloud. Make the cloud a size you can be somewhat comfortable with.

Now, manipulate this cloud of feelings. Make the cloud containing your emotions go farther away from you. Make the cloud go back down to the scene. Have the cloud rise high, then left and right. Realize the mastery you have with this cloud containing your feelings.

As you stay with the feeling-cloud manipulation, you are inviting your body at the parasympathetic level to begin to return to a less fearful state. You are calling your awareness out of your feelings and into an objective mind, just by mentally pushing the cloud around. In this way, you redial your chemistry. You will likely notice that it becomes easier to hold the image of the cloud because your body is beginning to send even more oxygen to your brain.

Step 2. Notice the Cloud Coming, Passing Through, and Going

You may have gotten all the relief you hoped for by practicing Step 1. If so, excellent. Your work is done here. If you still feel anxious, Steps 2 and 3 offer benefits beyond Step 1.

The cloud coming

When you're ready, invite the cloud containing your difficult feelings to rise up to eye level, but still at a distance. See the cloud there, at eye level, a comfortable distance away. At this point, the cloud and your feelings are still out there, far away.

Now, at your command, have the cloud of feelings begin to approach you from the front. Take this at your own pace. As the cloud of your feelings begins to approach, allow yourself to experience the difficult emotions the cloud contains, but only mildly. The cloud is still away from you, but coming closer. Describing this you might say, "Oh, I'm starting to feel a little uncomfortable as the cloud approaches."

You are now beginning to Read The Edges of your emotions. This is a tool useful in managing any difficult feeling. It readies you to regulate your emotions, rather than your emotions regulating you.

Use your mastery to manage how close you let the cloud of feelings approach. The closer the cloud gets, the more you experience those difficult emotions. The farther away the cloud, the less you experience the feelings contained there.

The cloud passing through

At your beckoning, have the cloud of your emotions make contact with and pass through you. See yourself as a big window screen, if that helps. As the cloud passes through, the difficult feelings contained there will feel more and more intense, until the emotions reach their most intense level.

At this point, you will feel the most uncomfortable. Have the cloud continue to pass through you. If you want the cloud and its emotions to move through you more quickly, imagine perhaps a big wind clearing them. Or you might imagine someone behind you, pulling the cloud through and out of you. Let your mind create whatever image it needs to manage the cloud of difficult emotions in the way that helps you the most. Your thoughts as the cloud passes through might be, "Oh, this is brutal. It's almost impossible to stay with these feelings."

Noticing the passing through of the cloud is the toughest part. It means standing in the presence of your difficult emotions, full on. Remember, *you are not your fear.* Keep some part of you outside the emotions, as an objective witness to it all. It's like watching a movie, but the movie is you.

The cloud going

You did it. You noticed your trauma or anxiety coming and passing through you. Keep noticing. Notice how the cloud is thinning out, now that it's almost completely through you. Thoughts about the cloud going could sound like this: "OK, I don't feel quite as uncomfortable or anxious as I did a few minutes ago. I'm still somewhat uncomfortable, but I think it's better." Keeping the image alive like this keeps you mindful. The mindfulness helps keep more blood and oxygen in your brain. That breaks the grip of the anxiety.

Now see the cloud fully behind and away from you, and take note of the difference in the intensity of your emotions. The farther the cloud gets from you, the less you feel the difficult emotions contained there, and the more comfortable you become.

Notice that the sense of trauma or anxiety may not be as severe as it was when you started the exercise: "Oh, you know what, I don't feel as scared as I did twenty minutes ago." By noticing over time all these changes in your feeling state, you begin to give your difficult emotions a form. Every form has a beginning, a middle, and an end. By working with your traumatic experience or anxiety in this way, you give it a form. It then no longer seems omnipresent, unruly, all-powerful, and unending. It, too, has a beginning and end. Your fear will become just your fear. Many who have tried this process report a sense of relief in feeling separate from the fear. It is still fear, but achieving distance from it seems to weaken its power. That returned power can now serve you.

With time and practice, you will likely notice that the clouds come and go a little quicker. Then you might notice that the clouds come less often. Be patient. Changing your internal landscape like this may take some time. With time, the mind becomes like blue sky full of clarity, calm, expansiveness and unlimited potential.

Step 3. Notice the Light Between the Clouds

The more you notice the light between the clouds, the more power you give the light. What's that mean? The first two steps of this technique have encouraged you to give your difficult emotions full attention, while they are present. This last step promotes the idea that it is equally important to give full attention to what's present when your fear isn't—the peace, the inner spaciousness, the absence of difficult emotions, the light between the clouds.

Between every cloud, there is light. Most people prefer light to darkness. However, when regularly dealing with difficult emotions, it's easy to forget to notice the light. In an anxious, uncomfortable emotional state, it's easy to overlook the absolute knowledge that there are periods, however brief, when the clouds part, the difficult emotions wane, and light is visible. There's a second of clarity or peace or trust.

Anxiety and peace, darkness and light, cloudy and clear—these are all simply states of mind. They are not enemies or allies. When one state is seen as good, the other is automatically established as evil or wrong or unhealthy. The task then becomes overcoming the enemy.

Fear is not an enemy. It's just a state of mind. Fighting it tends to give it power. On the other hand, Reading The Edges of fear or any difficult emotion in an unattached, non-reactive way drains it of power, and then you feel better.

In the same way, when you notice that your mind is calm or peaceful or trusting, that peaceful state gains power. When you give full attention to the fact that you are not having difficult emotions right now, the pleasantness expands. So noticing the light between the clouds becomes a sort of anxiety prevention. Your thoughts when noticing the light can sound something like this: "Man I feel good. My brain has slowed down. I'm actually aware of what's going on right this minute. I'm back."

A Next Step Approach

Let's say your home was heavily damaged by a hurricane a year ago and each time it storms you feel anxious. In the past year, by practicing the three steps just outlined, you've mastered the art of Reading The Edges. So now, when the rain whips and storms blow, you don't get nearly as fearful as you did. Excellent. At this point, you might want to try this:

As soon as your thoughts begin to induce fear when it becomes windy, notice them as you did above, and then transform them. You can do this by comfortably imagining that the fearful thoughts are infused with light, love, peace, or all of the above. Take a breath. See the fearful thoughts filling with light or love. Let this transformation visualization unfold naturally.

As this transformation happens, gently introduce thoughts based on your true experience: "There have been many windy days since the hurricane, but none of the winds caused damage. I still feel some anxiety when I hear the wind, but I have been safe. I'm going to let these inaccurate thoughts about the wind blend with my peace." In this way, you may transform the anxiety.

Early attempts at this, especially if you haven't mastered previous steps, can be frustrating. But it might work well for you right from the start. Experiment. Use what works. With practice, the transformation approach may give you the power to shift your anxiety quickly. If nothing else, replace the scary thoughts as best you can with just a blank or neutral mind.

It's a curious process and feeling. Strong, clear, disciplined, and accurate thoughts can transform the anxiety when blended with compassion or hope. At times, there may be a sensation of internal fortification that you can almost sense, followed by the soft edges of peace and relaxation.

This inner state parallels the experience of love. And when we reside in the feeling [not the thought] of love, we access all that is good and powerful and profound.

Clearing the clouds of trauma and anxiety entails moving through the difficult emotions, rather than around. It is transforming rather than resisting. It means knowing that it is possible to have fear, but at the same time choose not to be afraid. Like living in the eye of the storm.

Cherish the light. Your hardship, your anxiety, are not you. You are so much more.

CHAPTER FIFTEEN

Potholes: Unexpected Emotions that Jar You

There comes a time in most long drives when you get sleepy behind the wheel. The road's not changing much. Stripes on the highway have a hypnotic affect, road signs get a little blurry and your head starts to bob. Hopefully you pull off the highway and rest. If not, something may snap you out of the sleepiness.

So it is with the hardship journey. From what you can tell, the worst of your hardship pain is behind you. The road ahead is not as threatening as it once seemed. Everything's OK.

Maybe it's been years since the traumatizing event, or maybe many months. At any rate, your life has moments that actually feel normal. Old routines for work, kids' activities and neighborhood functions have returned.

Thankfully and most importantly, you're feeling better. Family and friends have adjusted to the new you. Everybody's looking and acting more like their old selves. Some of the pleasures of life are coming out of hibernation.

Early parts of the journey had you awake and alert, either as the survivor or support person—so much to do and to learn. Any potholes on your road were skillfully avoided. Eyes were wide open then, and you noticed almost everything.

However, now that you've been on the highway awhile, and things are OK, you're lulled into a bit of a trance. It's when you are in this mental and emotional state of relative relaxation that you might hit a pothole.

For some whose bodies have been changed by a physical trauma, the jolt comes in the form of a glance. It's the sideways and unexpected glimpse of your scar in the mirror. Just like that, you're bowled over by a wave of emotions, thoughts, and internal experiences. Where is all this feeling coming from? The sight of your own body or your loved one's body has triggered a domino of reactions you weren't ready for. All the old fears seem as strong as ever. Or maybe a wave of anger comes on. Maybe it's sadness—sadness that you, your body, your loved one's body, your spirit, and your family had to go through so much. And just like that, you are unmistakably back on the highway of the journey beyond hardship.

Kevin suffered a significant chemical burn to his face working in the garage. Immediately after surgery, his speech and appearance were both affected. He got through those times grateful to be alive and aware that more plastic surgery would return most of his speech and appearance. They did. The post-surgery facial scar was strong, but Kevin was patient as the scar healed and became less visible. In group, he shared, "I'm glad to be here, to be breathing like you do, and looking forward to the rest of my life. This accident, odd as it may seem, has been a gift to me. My wife and I got closer through it. This scar is the least of my worries."

Months went by. Kevin spoke in group about family issues, job issues, and what he was doing to take care of himself. Every once in a while, he would refer to his scar: "I'm fine with this. How I look is not a big deal."

One day Kevin came to group with a different message. "My wife and I had a portrait taken," he explained. "No big deal, right? Well, when the proofs showed up this week something really hit me."

After a long pause, someone in the group asked, "What happened, Kevin?"

"It's hard to talk about. I'm not exactly sure. All I know was when I saw myself in those pictures, something broke in me. My wife had to pull the pictures away. I went kinda crazy."

Kevin needed a couple of sessions to discover what had happened. Early in his journey, Kevin's anger was too powerful to be acknowledged. Some part of him knew that. Back then, Kevin developed other tools for getting through all that was being asked of him. This is a variety of the emotional efficiency discussed previously. But now that the rest of his life was getting back to normal, Kevin had the strength to look into the face of his anger. The anger was strong, but so was Kevin, and eventually he got beyond even his intense anger. Seeing himself in those portraits was a pothole for Kevin.

A similar emotional busting open can be created by what we might call *resemblance potholes*. You are cruising along at a pretty good clip with your recovery, you think. The pothole, however, is there, perhaps at the market when you hear the voice of a man that resembles the voice of the man who assaulted you. The fear that hits you out of nowhere is so strong you almost get sick. You drop your groceries and make your way to your car. There, shaking, you are painfully aware that you are still on the recovery road.

Scent provides the most powerful of memories, and the fragrance of a passing woman in the mall nearly brings you to your knees because it's the same perfume your late wife wore. That's a pothole.

One final circumstance that may be a pothole for some: everyone else's perfect life. This pothole has an odd shape. You're happy. So, too, are those you love. Then one day, pop—you're combing through a pile of emotions that sound like this: "My life isn't the same. I'm not the same. I didn't ask for this. All these people on TV, all my neighbors, so many of my family, they don't have a care in the world. But I have this mess in my head that hardship caused." This hidden resentment is a pothole.

Potholes can show up years after a traumatic life event, though not everybody hits these potholes. Even the folks who eventually travel forward from hardship with gladdened hearts can hit sharp pockets of feelings they don't or can't predict. Knowing that potholes are out there may make your journey beyond a little safer.

CHAPTER SIXTEEN

Road Weary: Compassion Fatigue for Helping Professionals

L ike a deep road weariness, emotional exhaustion can affect those in the helping professions—paramedics, psychotherapists, clergy, policemen, firefighters, doctors and nurses. Survivors of hardship and their support people can know this level of emotional fatigue, as well, but the focus in this chapter is on the professionals that serve people who have been traumatized.

This exhausted feeling often comes for helping professionals with the thought that there's no end to the highway. Everyday, they stand in the presence of other people's pain. They always know that tomorrow will be much the same.

The "I'm done" feeling for nurses can register mid-afternoon with the thought, "I can't stick a needle in one more patient today." Or for the exhausted policeman in the middle of the night thinking, "I can't show up for another shooting." Or for the counselor late in the day that hears inside, "I don't have it in me to calm a second suicidal client this evening." All these reactions could be signs of secondary post traumatic stress or compassion fatigue.

Compassion fatigue, as explained below, is not the same as burnout. Here are examples describing the principle differences based on Dr. Charles R. Figley's keystone book, *Compassion Fatigue: Secondary Traumatic Stress Disorders from Treating the Traumatized:*[13]

- Burnout comes from ongoing dissatisfaction. For example, when helping professionals face repeated hassles because of company policy, staff shortages, or time crunches. On the other hand, compassion fatigue is born of trauma, like the pain a surgeon might feel after regularly telling families their loved ones have suddenly lost consciousness.

- Burnout is usually slow to build. Like the ongoing frustration a qualified professional may feel about low pay in a not-for-profit organization. Compassion fatigue, however, comes on very quickly and intensely. Like the jolt a chaplain feels, taken in the arms of a father yelling out in sheer despair.

- Thoughts related to burnout may be persistent but not intrusive: "The constant headaches with this insurance company are making me crazy," or, "I just can't keep covering these twelve hour shifts." Thoughts related to compassion fatigue, on the other hand, are intrusive and can feel like stabs in the heart. Such thoughts have the power to break concentration, rest, and conversations. These intrusive thoughts are often accompanied by images. For example, distracted by replays of his day pulling children from their burning school, a firefighter driving home almost crashes.

- People feeling burnout usually commiserate. Couples dealing with a layoff may talk at dinner about how they're going to get through. Paramedics may share their concerns about overtime as they drive together. But people experiencing compassion fatigue often keep their startling images and thoughts to themselves: "If my boss knew I had thoughts like this about the people we take care of, I'd be canned," or "I'm a doctor. I'm supposed to be strong and available." Consequently, those dealing with compassion fatigue feel isolated and often withdraw, cutting themselves off from life-giving support.

In his book, Dr. Figley outlines many symptoms apparent in helping professionals dealing with compassion fatigue. These symptoms fall under six major categories and may include the following: perfectionism, self-doubt, minimization, numbness, nightmares, somatic reactions, loss of purpose, mistrust, intolerance and loneliness, among others.

Progressive organizations provide programs designed to aid their staff in minimizing and managing these symptoms. Employers of helping professionals can make a difference by acknowledging that compassion fatigue is real. The benefits of organizational interventions are obvious for the mental health of the helping professionals. But the organizations also gain from reduced turnover and training costs, higher productivity and quality service.

CHAPTER SEVENTEEN

Rest Stop #6: A Quick-Release Anxiety Tool—"I Am More Than My Fear"

Potholes on the journey beyond, whether hit by the helping professional, hardship survivor or support person, often come with rapid-onset anxiety. It might be the rush of panic when legal documents related to your tragedy arrive at your door. Or the racing mind when you or the one you love finds a new pain or bump months after cancer treatment. Time on the journey makes these difficult moments more bearable, as experience teaches you the usefulness of gently being less reactive. But fear is powerful. The following exercise is offered as a tool to help rapidly release you from fear.

"I Am More Than My Fear"

Step 1. State What You Observe

Each of us has stress activated signals (SAS) that mark the onset of anxiety. When used effectively, these signals can help us manage that anxiety. First, identify your specific mental and physical SAS—those cues that tell you anxiety may be starting. Try to identify the one SAS that shows up earliest. Perhaps when you first become anxious, your hands sweat or your heart beats faster. For some, the SAS may be nervous laughter or a rolling stomach.

Once you know what your first SAS is, let it inform you that anxiety is beginning. Watch for it. As soon as you recognize this cue in yourself, state what you observe. For example, say to yourself, "Oh, my mouth's getting dry. I can feel that. I know I'm starting to get anxious." This simple act of thinking helps to physiologically interrupt the fear-based fight or flight reaction in your body. This is another version of Reading The Edges—noticing the beginning of your fear.

Step 2. Declare, "I Am More Than My Fear"

Once you've observed the early signs of anxiety in yourself, declare, "I am more than my fear." Say it out loud if you want. With this declaration, you are creating within yourself the opportunity for something other than fear. Any time you observe your fear in such a way, you step outside that fear. In this way, you step into who you really are: the one observing the fear.

Step 3. Breathe Life into the Rest of You

So there you are: your fear and the rest of you. Leave the fear be. Notice it, but don't try to make the fear go away by pushing against it. It will push back, and you could get stuck in the struggle. Instead, breathe life into the rest of you. Take a deep breath, and imagine your breath traveling to an aspect of yourself that you wish to expand, or feel more fully. Maybe you want to feel more trusting. So, as you inhale, see your breath going to, expanding, and giving life to the trust you know exists inside you. You know this because you've felt trust before. Breathe life into your trust.

Perhaps you want to breathe life into more than your trust. So be it. See that happening. The number of qualities, feelings, or attributes you can expand far outnumber the fear. Fear isn't bad. It's just a small and sometimes powerful part of the total you. As a matter of fact, Joseph Hiller claims, "Fear is excitement without breath."

So, breathe life into as much of the rest of you as you like. See the breath going to all those other aspects of you, making them open or grow. If you like, see the rest of you dancing. Notice the fear, and invite the rest of you to shine.

CHAPTER EIGHTEEN

Crashes and Getting Stuck in Traffic: Major Interruptions in Your Recovery Journey

The more time you spend on the highway, the more likely you are to have an accident or get stuck in traffic. While detours and potholes slow your progress, crashes and traffic can bring your travels to a stop.

Crashes

<u>Multiple Losses</u>: Losing more than one person in the same tragedy such as a natural disaster, fire, shooting or auto accident, has to be the most difficult of hardships. The pain from this kind of trauma is almost unfathomable and the healing a lengthy journey.

Similarly, it can be a long recovery road when one loss is followed closely by the death of a second loved one. It's very tough to pick yourself back up after a second loss when you're still healing from the first.

When multiple losses are experienced, *complicated grief* is usually involved. People suffering complicated grief take longer to heal, understandably. Fundamentally, the grief process is protracted and sometimes stalls.

<u>Recurrence</u>: The emotional, mental, and relational pain caused by recurrence can be severe for all involved. For the survivor, feeling emotionally whole after a recurrence can be difficult. The words, "The disease has come back," cut deep. There's a treacherous sense of powerlessness, despair and terror.

Hope is the biggest piece in this pained puzzle. It's hard to recover hope with a second occurrence of an illness. For many who experience recurrence, hope does not recur as sure, as fast or as strong: "The more you hope, the harder you fall." The same fear of hoping may strike the caregiver or invade the helping professional's spirit.

<u>Relapse</u>: Whether it is chemicals, porn, binge eating or gambling, addictions are hardships. Freeing yourself is a huge accomplishment. But if you've successfully released yourself from overuse only to have the addiction take hold again, you too may feel profoundly hopeless. Relapse is surely a crash on the hardship recovery road.

When hardship includes multiple loss, recurrence or relapse, many find mustering the strength to go forward very difficult. In these situations, tremendous patience is important for all involved. There is a level of emotional fragility in each circumstance that is extremely difficult to comprehend. Dreams are dashed. Of course, they can be rebuilt, but doing so is especially trying.

Relationships may be contorted at this time. The survivor feels like anything but a survivor. It's easy to feel victimized. When that happens, many tough questions can arise: "Have I done something wrong?" "Will I have the strength to go on?" "Do I want to?" "Will staying with it make a difference?" "Where is God?" "What's the point of all this?" The caregiver is asking many of these same questions.

Try not to let the questions scare you. They're just thoughts. Convert the fearful thoughts to thoughts that comfort you, if you can. Why not? Give yourself permission to feel whatever you feel. See dark emotions as passing clouds. They may be powerfully intense, but they are still only feelings. The rest of you is there. Hold on to whatever gives you strength, if that's what you decide.

No more net: When important people leave you, when jobs change, when you move from a comfortable neighborhood, when treatment stops or when you lose anything that feels like primary support, you might crash.

Even when the reason for the change is positive, like a better job, or the remission of your disease, fear can show up. This fear may be confusing. A better job or the successful end of treatment is a time when those around the survivor applaud. Generally, everybody's pretty up. Fear in the survivor at this point can be met with the question, "How can you feel bad at a time like this?" No safety net.

If you've been dealing with real hardship for any reason, support may be the one thing you counted on and the thing that got you through. People, places, groups and even treatment itself become a kind of lifeline for hardship survivors. When that lifeline is severed for any reason, the rush of unexpected emotions is enough to cause a crash.

<u>Emotional Unpacking</u>: There's one more major cause of crashes, and this one can be perplexing: emotional unpacking. Previously we spoke of emotional packing—putting away the emotions that can come in the early part of the hardship journey, so full attention may be given to matters at hand. But what is packed must be unpacked. When and how the unpacking happens can be unsettling.

Joan joined a group nearly eight months after her hardship event. Life, by her report, was returning to normal: "Mom, are you going to take me to practice?" and, "Honey, we're going to dinner with Bob and Cindy Friday night, OK?" Not OK. For some reason, nothing felt OK to Joan. Not long after joining the group, Joan made contact with her disappointment. At first she couldn't figure it out. Then it started to become clear.

Joan felt that everybody wanted everything to be just like it used to be. At some level, so did Joan. But at another level, she knew it would never be and she was disappointed at people pressing her to be the mother, wife, friend, and person she no longer was.

Joan felt that family and friends acted as if nothing ever happened. Joan knew she couldn't be the same person she used to be. Too much had impacted her body, mind, and spirit. Joan resented the fact that people started giving her the "get over it" message: "Look, I know it was hard on you, but things are better now, and you're fine. Thank goodness. Let's put it behind us."

But just as everyone else was ready to move on, Joan was finding the energy to face feelings she couldn't early on, like fear and sadness and anger. The last thing she felt she could do was put it all behind her. In group, she began opening what felt to her like a whole suitcase full of tough emotions.

Joan did great through the initial throes of her hardship. She got back on her horse and started to ride. Then it hit. All the feelings that had been packed in the beginning of her journey were now busting out, begging to be unpacked, and a few other feelings had been added along the way. This unpacking may happen months, and even years, after a tragedy.

The survivor isn't the only one completely taken off guard by this unpacking process. Everybody in the family is baffled by the survivor's emotionality at this time. Understanding comes in handy here. Sometimes it's the survivor who wants to act as if nothing ever happened, leaving support people in a quandary.

Getting Stuck in Traffic

Sitting in traffic is no fun under any circumstance, but it's especially frustrating when you've got somewhere to be. Getting stuck on the healing journey can feel much worse than any traffic jam. Where you are feels awful. Where you want to be looks better, but you just can't get there. When you feel emotionally, mentally or relationally stuck, there seems to be no way out. You've tried everything you know, but you just can't feel better in your head. There may be brief periods when the traffic moves, only to be followed by long spells of sitting idly again.

We all feel as if we're spinning our wheels sometimes. But feeling really stuck is not the same and can be a very dark place. It's like all the cars on the highway have broken down with no exit ramp in sight. The mind sees no way out, and the heart follows. You want desperately to get better, but somehow that desire can't break through to the point of change: "Why can't I stop acting like this?" or "What's it going to take to get me to stop thinking this way?" or "When will I be able to treat other people differently?"

Here's a definition of stuckness that might help explain why you can't move forward, even when that's truly what you want.

Stuckness: the inability to tolerate your own will
because it echoes the will
of someone who over-controlled you
in the past.

For the sake of understanding, let's work with an example. Imagine that your hardship happened a year and a half ago. Early on, there were days you didn't think you could keep going. But you did. Then the clouds started to clear a bit, and you had days in a row that felt OK. Now, life actually is enjoyable at times. That's a tremendous journey in eighteen months.

As the chaos settled and the pain eased, you realized you gained weight following your trauma. It happens. You've been trying for a while to get back to a weight you're comfortable with, but it's been one step forward, two steps back. It's not the first time you've wrestled with your weight. Our culture's obsessed with appearance and weight. Regardless, you know the value of a healthy life style and your weight is more than you want it to be. Yet, it seems the harder you try, the more weight you gain. With mounting frustration, voices in your head are telling you to forget about it. This is stuckness.

To apply the stuckness definition, your *will* is to get back to a weight that feels right to you. The word "will" has some oomph to it. Will is not passive. It is not "noticing." It's doing. It has force— so much so that there's pop talk about willing things into being. Will can change things. Nothing wrong with will itself. However, because will can be so powerful, what someone does with the force of his or her will can either be highly useful or highly destructive: Mother Teresa versus Hitler.

If the people in your early life used their will in constructive ways with you, then you and your own will are likely on friendly terms. You have come to know through experience that strong and loving focus of behavior can create wonderful things. Consequently, you probably don't get stuck very often. You listen to your own will because you trust it has your best interest at heart, just like the people in your early life.

However, if the people in your early life used their will (consciously or not) to bend your will so you would better meet their emotional needs, with little awareness that you had needs as well, then you and your own will are likely at odds.

Why? Because will in any form has force. You were imprinted in a negative way by the force of the wills of the important people in your early life. When the force of your own will speaks to you, it feels to your psyche like the force of the people who lorded their will over you. So you resist it. In other words, you have an *inability to tolerate your own will.*

As a matter of fact, when you are stuck in this will loop, the harder you try, the more you resist the very thing you want. Seems odd, but the more forceful you become with yourself, the more your own will feels like the will of someone who hurt you. Since you were relatively powerless over your childhood caretakers, there wasn't much you could do about the situation. Actually, the situation was normal to you. But now, as your own caretaker, nobody can make you do anything. Not even yourself. You are stuck.

So, how to get unstuck? Read The Edges. Step back and look at the reality of things, and then speak lovingly to yourself till you get free. If you're trying to lose weight, gently observe yourself. When you take an extra piece of bacon, or go for another sliver of chocolate, just see yourself doing it. That's how it starts.

Once you've come to be an observer of even this in yourself, you can gradually shape your own behavior: "This morning I took that extra piece of bacon. I wanted to. Cool. Now I've got this dark chocolate bar in my hand. Do I really want to eat it? I can if I want. I've decided that I want to lose some weight. Hmmm. That's the voice of my will. My will is not trying to hurt or control me. It's got my back. OK, I'm gonna put the candy down."

After you put the chocolate down (or the new purse, or the beer, or the roulette ball, or the new sex partner) watch what happens. You might find you get angry, sad or even scared. There are deep dynamics at work when you try to make this kind of change. If you keep listening to what's happening under the feelings, you may uncover beliefs that have misguided you.

Here's what this all might sound like in your mind: "OK, I didn't have that chocolate. Now I'm starting to feel agitated. Oohhh. I'm mad! Wow. I'm mad because I deserve chocolate. I'm a good enough person. Chocolate makes me feel better. It's really the only thing that does." In Reading The Edges you've uncovered some great information about yourself. First of all, you do deserve chocolate. You've realized that when you don't get it, you don't feel cared for. So chocolate makes you feel cared for.

This information may make it easier to listen to your will the next time you want chocolate because you realize the strong desire for it is connected to you feeling valued. You could decide to care for yourself just because—to really love yourself just the way you are, with or without chocolate. Or you could put other things in place that line up with your will to lose weight that also help you feel valued. Exercise, as an example. Or the simple fact that you listened to your own will, and put the chocolate down might help you feel valued.

As you gain the ability to be loving and strong with yourself, the traffic starts to move. Soon you're making your way, and the ride is smoother.

Emotional Efficiency

What is *emotional efficiency*? Joan had unconsciously practiced emotional efficiency at the start of her journey. Some part of her knew that venturing deep into all the feelings generated by her tragedy was more than she could handle right then. Her entire self chose to pack the emotional stuff away to be unpacked later. Later usually becomes a time when things are better and settling down for the survivor. It's as if the entire person knows when it's safe to take this unpacking task on.

Here's another version of emotional efficiency. Sarah was surviving cancer and struggling to finish her treatment. Pain and fatigue were significant. In addition, Sarah had just made it through a nasty divorce and her ex-husband was not helping. Besides that, her young daughter was developmentally disabled. When Sarah began in the counseling group, she came with rage wrapped in lots of anxiety. Her greatest anxiety was about dying and opening the door for her ex to gain custody of their child. For months she used the group to download her anxiety and anger. Then one week Sarah seemed different. There was an air of peace about her.

The group asked Sarah about her change: "I can't afford to be anxious any more." She went on to explain that when really anxious and angry, her pain got out of control, and when that happened, she couldn't feel any joy with her daughter. That simple awareness changed her life. Anxiety and anger registered now as wasteful. She had developed another sort of *emotional efficiency*.

In this chapter we've focused on situations along the journey beyond hardship that are especially troubling and painful: crashes and getting stuck in traffic. In both cases, hope is at a premium. When hope is hard to come by, depression can sneak in. The next chapter offers a tool for working through depression.

CHAPTER NINETEEN

Rest Stop #7: Feeding the Hungry Ghost—An Exercise for Responding to Depression

Crashing or getting stuck, discussed in the previous chapter, can create bouts with depression. In our culture, depression is generally considered something to avoid—an enemy. Yes, depression is difficult. Yes, serious and chronic depression may require professional support and even medication. But what would happen if you thought of depression as a messenger of sorts? What would change if you pushed less against this experience and instead made some room for it?

Make no mistake about it. Some feel their depression is the worst pain they have ever experienced. In many cultures there's little training for responding to sadness, fear, hurt, hopelessness, and anger. Consequently, these emotions are often avoided. But pain resisted becomes suffering. Avoided emotions underpin depression.

Acknowledging your tough feelings sooner, mitigates depression. This particular exercise helps shift your perception of depression as an *enemy* to depression as an *informant*. An informant often appears as the enemy, but eventually shares useful information.

When perceived as an enemy, depression becomes something to fight or appease. People who see depression as the enemy act in ways designed to keep this difficult emotion quiet; to keep it at bay and in check. These people were probably taught this pattern by important adults in their young lives who themselves never learned how to respond to tough feelings. Pushing depression away is part of our culture. But unfortunately, the one who "appeases" the crocodile, as Winston Churchill put it, is simply the last one eaten.[14]

So, how can you respond to depression besides appeasing it? What else can you do when you begin to experience that darkness—the feeling that you just can't get happy? Here's the story of the Hungry Ghost to answer that question.

In Tibet, children are taught to carry a grain of rice in their pockets. The rice, children are told, is to be thrown into the mouth of the Hungry Ghost, should it approach. The Hungry Ghost is depicted having rows and rows of razor sharp teeth in gaping jaws. So what good is a grain of rice? Legend has it that when you throw a single grain of rice into the fierce jaws of the Hungry Ghost, its mouth immediately closes, revealing a tiny body capable of consuming nothing more. The child's scary emotions of fear, sadness, and disappointment are represented by the monster and all its teeth.

In applying this story to adults with depression, the Tibetan wisdom is clear: when responding to difficult emotions, it helps to face them and then nurture them in some way. Only after acknowledging and nurturing these emotions can you discover what is true—the feelings feared are only a perceived monster. These poignant emotions only have the power they are given.

With this notion in mind, here are three steps for dealing with depression, especially in its early stages. People with serious or prolonged depression should consult a professional.

Feeding the Hungry Ghost: An Exercise for Responding to Depression

Step 1. Face Your Own Discomfort

The first step in responding to depression is to face your own discomfort. To do this, you usually have to slow down enough to make contact with your discomfort. And just like the Tibetan child who is invited to look into the jaws of the Hungry Ghost, looking into the eyes of your own pain may be very scary.

Slowing down may mean doing less of the things you've done to keep the pain at bay. Maybe that means exercising less, or feeling other people's emotions less, or controlling another's behavior less, or spending less time in the office, or shopping less, or eating less, or any of the many other drugging actions that can numb emotional pain. Stopping these actions in yourself is a monumental task, especially if it's how you've managed the pain most of your life. The stronger your hidden, difficult emotions are, the more forceful are your actions to numb those emotions.

Be patient with yourself. There's a reason you don't want to feel what's in you. As you slow down and begin to thaw, all that you have been anesthetizing yourself against will start to smart. You may need some counsel at this point. At the very least, it will help to talk to your mate or a close friend. Journaling is useful, too.

Step 2. Nourish It with Your Attention

Once you're facing your own discomfort, you can now set an intention in your heart, mind, or spirit. You can do this through prayer, or meditation, or simple silence. In responding to depression, your intention might be to gain awareness of what's at the center of your pain. In a sense, you now seek to understand the depression by offering it your attention. Ask yourself over the next couple of weeks to simply notice your inner life. There's nothing to change or do at this point. If you make this process of attention "an assignment," you set yourself up to get an "A" or an "F," and that may cause more pain. Instead, just notice.

Invite the non-judgmental observer within you to simply witness what seems to be true. For instance, how often do you feel the depression and what, when, where, or how does it tend to get stronger? What core feelings live inside the depression: anger, sadness, hopelessness, hurt, disappointment, terror? How much territory do the feelings claim in your emotional landscape? Does that change? How old is the part of you that seems to be having the tough emotions? If you had to say, where do the feelings show up in your body: your head, your chest, your belly? Is this a place you have physical ailments? There are no right or wrong answers. There is no task to master. You just want to get to know this sad part of yourself a bit better. You are nourishing the depression with your attention.

Step 3. Listen for Information

Now that you've slowed down and nourished your depression by paying more attention to it, your depression might have a message for you. It may want to be an informant. Listen.

Deep within you there is a part that is very wise and understands more than you might believe. That wisdom is best heard when you still yourself and earnestly wait for understanding. Wait is the operant word here. Let the understanding come to you. This may take time. Your dreams might kick up as you slow down. They can teach about the depression, too.

In listening to your depression with that wisest part of who you are, you may discover that your depression is much older than your hardship. In the quiet, you perhaps remember that when you were seven years old you were having pains in your gut just like the pain you feel now. Maybe that awareness reveals a very important connection between how you interacted with others then and how you interact with others now.

As an example, through listening, perhaps you realize for the first time that you aren't always blue. You're only blue after spending time with certain people. More listening reveals that those people find fault with you. Slowly, you see those people less, and your depression lifts. Then your gut feels better.

Maybe you listen deeply and discover that you haven't paid attention to your own instincts about what's best for you during the hardship. So, you make time to talk with your spouse about this, and together switch things up. A few days later, you notice that you feel less depressed.

Through practice of the three steps offered in this exercise, you will likely learn that the closer attention you pay to your emotional experience, including your depression, the more it can teach you. Respect it. It is not an enemy. It's an informant.

CHAPTER TWENTY

Road Rage: Understanding Anger

Anybody who's been on the road long enough is bound to have a flare-up or two. You get uncomfortable away from home so long, you want to get off the road, you're tired and on your last nerve. Everybody in the car knows it and probably feels much the same way. With enough detours and potholes and potential crashes during the journey beyond hardship, there could be some anger. The truth is, many people wrestle with the emotion of anger, whether or not they are surviving hardship. Like the general population, many hardship survivors have an all or nothing relationship with their own anger.

Recognizing Hidden Anger

"I don't even know what anger feels like," Francie reflected. "I get scared and sad and disappointed, but I don't get angry. I guess I don't know how to get angry," she admitted, sounding both sad and surprised at the same time. Francie was thirty-eight when she lost her business to a fire. Her parents lived nearby, but the relationship with them was strained. Though she had some friends, Jack, her boyfriend, was her closest ally.

In the beginning, Jack stood by her. However, that relationship thinned. And five months into our work together, Francie found out that Jack was seeing someone else. While this loss was extremely painful, it provided Francie a way to befriend her anger.

"Francie, you've openly described how hurt you are by Jack," I began one session. "You've also told me nothing makes sense anymore. What other emotional or physical reactions have you noticed over the past week?"

"It's weird," she said, "that you ask about physical reactions. My stomach's been a wreck the last couple days."

"How is your stomach right now?" was my next question.

"Not good, why?"

"Well," I answered, "maybe your stomach has something to say to you."

With this as the introduction, Francie began a venture into her own anger. Unaware of what was happening internally, she kept a log of what was going on in her stomach, her mind, and her emotions. In the weeks that followed, Francie began to make connections that slowly surfaced hidden anger. First, she dug through bitter resentment at Jack. Under this anger, Francie found resentment about the fire and its devastation. And then under that anger, Francie discovered a part of herself that was nearly rageful. This deeper, older anger, however, had little to do with her boyfriend or her situation. Through this process, Francie's emotional congestion was beginning to clear, and so was her spirit.

The best way to clear the congestion of any emotion is through it, not around it. Well-meaning purveyors of advice often suggest that anger is a bad emotion and should be avoided. But the very act of avoiding emotion creates congestion. Like any difficult emotion, when anger is acknowledged and accepted, new action rises up naturally. Working with anger, you learn of its guiding force, and you consequently create a life that is more comfortable. And in this new life, as we will see later in the chapter, you may find yourself feeling less and less anger, genuinely, and not from going around it but from going through it.

Who Is to Blame?

Before we discuss how emotional congestion may occur, it's important to talk about blame. There is none. Not of significant people in your past. Not of parents. Not of you. We all do, and have done, the best we can. Blame is of no good to anyone. This discussion of anger is about understanding. The heart carries the past. That past can be wonderful and filled with love, and that comes through in all the relationships you have today. Your past may also have involved other encounters and circumstances that left a wound on your heart—it's the human condition. That wound also comes through in all the relationships you have today.

However, our goal is to move forward. When you understand how wounds of the past influence experiences of the present, you position yourself to create a better future. This instinctive healing process flows naturally from understanding.

Understanding Anger

So, what's behind the widespread struggles with the emotion of anger? Put simply, your early life environment may have taught you to keep your anger to yourself. Consequently, your anger may have gotten stuck inside you.

Many experience anger as full on or full off because that's what they saw from the important people in their young lives. Couples often pair around this anger equation. One has outbursts of anger, and the other allows it. Another way to think of it is that one member of the pair tends toward aggression and the other toward passivity. These tendencies are not gender specific.

We generally feel more accepting of passive behavior and judge aggressive behavior. Truth is, both aggressive and passive behavior can be powerful. Aggressive power simply tends to be more apparent, direct, and abusive. Passive power tends to be more difficult to identify, less direct, and more manipulative. We often see aggressive people as non-caring and passive people as caring. This may be inaccurate.

Anger at the level of rage is often inappropriate, destructive and brings violence into relationships and homes. Yet it is also clear that passive power can be insidious and difficult to heal from. But most importantly, both the aggressive and passive responses to anger send a very clear message to the young child growing up in this environment: "Anger is dangerous."

Anger is a powerful emotion and even when appropriately expressed, can feel *overpowering*—so overpowering that it may be misread as controlling. Of course, any time we think we're being controlled, we resist. This is the rub. If we think our healthy anger is seen as controlling to someone else, we may keep it to ourselves. Or if we think we're being controlled by someone else's healthy anger, we may tell them to put it away. Healthy anger that is thwarted may congest in the person that's angry. Suppressed and congested anger, as we discussed in Chapter 5, may compromise immune function.

So how did this dynamic play out in the life of a child whose anger is stuck inside as an adult? The aggressive parent may have been threatened by the child's anger. This may have been acted out in a way that scared or punished the child for his or her young anger. Consequently, the child heard literally or figuratively, "Don't you dare get angry with me!" The child's anger was not allowed and became stuck. The passive parent, by allowing the anger of his or her spouse, also said to the young one, "Keep your anger to yourself, like I do." The child's anger was encouraged to be withheld and thereby became stuck. Yes discipline has its place with children. But children have a right to likes and dislikes, and sometimes those get expressed through anger.

People who are threatened by, and therefore, thwart the healthy anger of others are usually carrying a lot of hurt and fear beneath their own anger. These people probably had their own young anger thwarted. People who passively allow the unhealthy anger of others probably witnessed that same allowance in an important relationship in their own lives. This is the anger cycle. In this cycle, there is a lot of fear. When fear is present, love is not. Sadly, love is what everyone wants and it is the one thing that can break the anger cycle. Actually, fear may be "the root of all evil," and love the solution.

The Self, Saying No, and Congested Anger

Countless survivors have said they never learned to say no. But saying no is a part of being human. Saying no is one way the self shows up. Saying no is usually queued up when we feel angry. When done appropriately, this expression of anger is very healthy and natural. Of course, healthy anger often just shows up in children, i.e., the terrible two's. It seems though, many individuals were never allowed or taught to pay attention to their anger and to say no; that is, their authentic self was given limited support.

Independent thinking, opinion expressing, and acknowledging one's own emotions are all ways the self emerges. "Baseball is boring," "I think the yellow shoes are prettier," "I don't like brussels sprouts," "You scared me," and "Stop tickling me," are all ways a child might give voice to the emerging self and say, "no." Often, these very expressions of self were discounted or ignored in the early lives of those who now struggle, as adults, with how to respond to their own anger. These are the seeds of congested anger.

The origins of congested, old anger take many forms. Not being allowed to express yourself with opinions, likes and preferences is to experience a type of neglect. This is not neglect in the traditional sense—all the essentials like shelter, food, clothing, and even love may have been provided. Instead, the neglect described here is more likely an unconscious act of suppression by important people in the young person's life.

As the young, emerging self with its anger was suppressed by significant others, and trained not to come out, that individual's anger and true self got stuck inside. But because anger is as natural as all the emotions, and occurs in everyone, what happens to the anger that is stuck inside?

There are two basic ways the stuck self, with its anger, manages this suppression. In one way, the anger gets turned in against the self. That's what *shame* is. The second way is anger that regularly boils over and turns out against others. These two reactions to anger held inside produce two types of adult personalities: the compliant "say-yes" person who tends to agree with and support others, or the aggressive "impose-yes" person who tends to demand agreement and support *from* others. There is always a third option. That option is the person who may agree with and support others and expresses very little anger, then explodes, and demands.

It makes sense that more of the compliant say-yes adults tend to suffer illness than the impose-yes adults. After all, in the say-yes population, there was no apparent permission to send natural anger outside the self. So instead, the anger got turned in against the self, and as we established earlier, this can be very hard on the body.

Consequences of Unexpressed Anger

In many survivors, consistently unexpressed anger can turn back on the self in the form of shame, self-rejection, or poor esteem, over time producing old anger. This old anger ferments, tears you up inside, and turns into resentment.

Adults who have not learned to say no, yet naturally desire mastery in their lives, often feel powerless. In response to that powerlessness, they may attempt to hyper-control their surroundings. This could be the person who is extremely neat or extremely driven professionally. It might be the adult who tries to feel everyone else's feelings as a way to quiet the need for control. It could be the adult whose humor comes at the expense of others. Or it might be the adult that pushes, criticizes, or over-manages, be it self, spouse, employee, or child.

Some who feel powerless attempt to feel mastery by having too much or too little food, too much or too little exercise, too much or too little sex, too much or too little structure, or too many techniques or substances to alter their mood. Unexpressed anger is not the only explanation for such behaviors, but it's often a piece of the puzzle.

With understanding, you may be more able to accept yourself and others. When you bring compassion in, growth naturally follows. Life gets better. Who knew anger could be a doorway to a full and pleasurable life? If we don't understand our reasons for anger, life feels anything but pleasurable.

People who never learned to say no often find themselves as adults in relationships that minimize them. How does this happen? These adults practice what they were taught: to say yes. That is, as children they learned it was safer, and they felt more valued when they agreed with the predominant opinion and kept their point of view to themselves. *In the adult, this say-yes behavior attracts others who need to hear yes.* Consequently, the self that got stuck inside the child remains stuck in the adult. In extreme cases, these adults with a self stuck inside may find themselves in abusive situations. The result is more hurt and more fear.

Those who never learned to say no are often trained as children to be friendly and helpful and respectful. Friendliness, helpfulness, and respectfulness are positive characteristics. However, when you add those qualities to an adult who has never learned to say no, difficulties may arise. On the outside, these adults appear happy and are fun to be around. They can be generous with their time and money. Yet, these same folks often agree to more than they really want: more work, more time, more donated money, more self-sacrificing. It's not uncommon for these people to work themselves sick and smile through it all. The adult is now repeating the childhood experience: the self is not being heard. Their resentment grows.

Life may not be easy for the impose-yes adult either. Often, these frustrated individuals add layers to their pain by their own actions, driving important people out of their lives with the intensity of their anger. The impose-yes adults are then left without the care and support that might heal their injured hearts.

Another way to say all this is that people who give and give and give often end up in relationships with people who take and take and take, and vice versa. These relationships may become abusive.

Comparatively, people who give and take often end up in relationships with people who give and take. These relationships may become balanced and healthy.

Whether turned in on the self as shame, or out against others as aggression, the person who never learned to say no travels with a lot of resentment. Louise Hay, an internationally recognized self-help author and lecturer, was diagnosed with cancer. Here is her take on illness and anger:

I knew cancer was a disease of deep resentment that has been held for a long time until it literally eats away at the body. I had been refusing to be willing to dissolve all the anger and resentment at "them" over my childhood. There was no time to waste; I had a lot of work to do.[15]

Befriending Your Anger

How does one make friends with anger? It starts by practicing the Triple A Exercise described in Chapter 6. By acknowledging the anger, the fear, the hurt, and the pain, you begin to invite the self to come out. The process can be very painful. Everything in you says, "Don't say it! Don't feel it!" Acknowledging and expressing your anger—your self—may have gotten you punished in some way as a little one. Like a shy turtle, you'll keep withdrawing from this acknowledgment. That's OK. Stay with it. Take your time. By giving yourself time and patience, you are retraining yourself. In this way, you begin to honor all of who you are and self-respect is born. Once this happens, authenticity emerges.

As you grow in authenticity, you begin to notice what you like and what you don't like; what you feel and what you don't feel; what you want to do and what you don't want to do: "I really don't like talking to Jay anymore, because all he does is complain," or, "Dang, I liked that show." The self is being breathed into. The self that was stuck inside is being born. How wonderful!

As you acknowledge and accept all that you are, you will act differently. People may not like that right away: "What happened to the person who was so easy to get along with, so friendly, and always said yes when you needed help?" Well, that person is still there. But now that person has opinions, with likes and dislikes. That person is taking better care of the self.

If you can, avoid the strong pull to return to being the person you used to be. Realize that your old self served you in the best way possible then. What you need now is something different, even if you're not exactly sure what that is. Keep venturing into the unknown with courage and what you seek will become apparent.

Eventually, people will adjust to the emergence of your self. Some will take it in stride. Some will leave you. Others will arrive who were not in your life before. These new friends actually like people who say no. They are attracted to people who know who they are and act on that in a way that is both respectful of self and others. In healthy relationships, each person can be strong without being aggressive, and caring without being passive.

Being kind to people who welcome your strength, your real self, is easy. It's also authentic. Authenticity cools the fire of resentment. True love of self and others emerges. Road rage becomes a thing of the past. The whole process breeds health.

Anger, Beliefs, and God

The power of your beliefs, whether or not they include some construct of a god or transpersonal force, may be impacted by your thoughts about those beliefs. What you believe is not at issue here. What's important is recognizing the impact of your *thoughts about your beliefs*, whatever the beliefs may be. Your thoughts about your beliefs can be either life-giving or life-taking. Your position on all things, including matters of spirit, and the related thoughts you assign to those beliefs, can either help and strengthen you or hinder you during your journey beyond hardship. Don't overlook that power. Be conscious and harness the power of your beliefs, whatever they are. Finding more power in the self often means visiting your anger that is holding the power.

For example, say you believe there is a deep guidance within you that is wise. Maybe you call that God or The True Self or simply the goodness of humankind. Since your hardship befell you, that belief may have flourished, and you cherish a profound connection with this inner goodness, or God, however you describe it. You see the presence of that power even in your pain. You can't escape its love. You know way down inside that your God, or this innate goodness, is powerfully on your side. In a sense, *your thoughts about your beliefs* are strengthening you. FYI, this is not just emotional and mental strengthening: it's physical, too. [16]

If you're a say-yes adult, your thoughts about your beliefs may not be so uplifting. You may be actually turning around the same beliefs that have strengthened others and pointing them against yourself, through your thinking. So let's say you do believe in God. But if you find it difficult to express your anger with people, it may be equally difficult to express anger at your God. Maybe you think God will punish you for that anger, so you can't express it or acknowledge it.

Once again, the self is getting stuck inside. You may even think that your hardship is a punishment from your God. This is a trick bag that's very tough to escape. At a time when you could use all the support available, a nurturing experience of a god has been taken out of the picture. Perhaps God has become a reflection of your human experience. In a sense, God is limited to what you think God is. In this case, *your thoughts about your beliefs* are working against you.

So, if you think God is punitive, *why not think another way*—a way that perhaps supports you? Why not think of God as loving every cell of who you are? Why not think that God, or that deep, wise part of you, enjoys your disagreements? Why not think that God proudly receives the strength of your anger and relishes the thought that you can feel so powerfully? Why not think that God has been waiting for you to be completely honest, to bring your whole self to its loving presence, so God can cradle all of you, so you can feel more loved than you knew possible? You can choose that.

This isn't about religious conversion or being born again—not in the conventional sense. Beliefs are simply chosen thoughts. If you have assigned a tremendous amount of power to some belief, or something, or someone, and then turn that power against yourself by what you think, why not use your thoughts to convert that power into something that helps you? Your thoughts are more powerful than you recognize. Remember the visualization research cited in Chapter 5?

How to Say No

Many survivors have said that recovery is self-care, not selfish. Saying no is about survival. Saying no is self-care.

When you cut your hand, the physical self doesn't ponder whether or not it should use its immune cells to repair the wound. The strong instinct to stay well, to take care of the self, happens automatically. Perhaps herein lays a message to the mental, emotional, and spiritual self. In essence, if you don't instinctively take care of the rest of your self, your emotions and mind may become ill and limited, just like the body would without a similar instinct.

Most great religions hold selflessness in high regard and teach us to love others as the self is loved. They teach that true happiness is found in this way of life. Something very subtle lies in these tenets that often seems underplayed and overlooked. These principles of selflessness assume that *one's self* is truly loved and treated well, FIRST!

Love starts with the self. The Golden Rule is not, "Love your self as you love your neighbor." It's, "Love thy neighbor as thyself." You love others only as well as you love yourself. If you love yourself well, you love others well. But if you don't love yourself well, you truly can't love others well.

Here's another way to think of it. If you consistently give your self away, who then is left to give? What do you give? We all have met people who seem hollow. They laugh but seem disconnected from their joy. They give but don't really seem present when they do—eyes distant, though looking right at you; mind without focus;

body almost hapless. In these people, the self has been completely given away. Even Buddha, Christ, and masters of the great religions found ways to nourish their own spirits: time alone, time in prayer, time being cared for by others, even time in anger.

Say a friend needs your help. If you can and want to help, great. But if your instinct in that moment is to rest and take time to be alone, then when you do so, you love thyself. Not doing so denies your instinct, and you lose a little part of you.

Yes, there are of course times when everyone gives when they don't want to. However, if you consistently ignore the voice of self-care, you will be injured. No one is responsible for your care but you. When you solidly acknowledge that fact, you begin creating rather than reacting in life.

When you create your life in this way, the sky's the limit. Giving by choice from the life you have created generates more life, and not just for you. Others can sense this difference. You're happier, more alive. Others' reactions to this kind of giving add life to yours. To create your life, you need skills in saying no.

To answer the question, "How do you say no?" consider first this question: "What happens when your bucket is empty?" When you have emptied yourself to the point of exhaustion, what do you do? Do you give some more? What does that give you: a sense of self, a sense of mastery, a sense of control, a sense of satisfaction, a sense of safety because you aren't sure what else to do when asked to give? The Need Theorists tell us that all our behavior is motivated by some need. In other words, if you always say yes, there is some benefit in that for you. Acknowledge what that benefit is, and accept yourself completely for it. It's not a matter of good or bad. It's simply who you are today.

If you can identify *the need*, you may then be able to find more direct ways to meet it—ways without the potential toll on the self. Selflessness has its own reward, but if there is no self left, then there is no real gift either. Many people give because they have learned no other way of being. The giving then becomes rote, and rote giving is not really a choice. Their gift is, therefore, not really a gift. When we learn to say no, giving becomes a choice, and then it truly is a gift.

One of the best ways to learn to say no is to first listen deeply to the self. Listen for what you really need or want, in all situations. Lots of people don't know how to do this. The focus in early life for these people was always outside the self—what others expected, felt, needed, or wanted. Tuning into the self in this way takes patience and love. Start with little things like, "What time do I really like to go to bed?" or, "Do I like to be the passenger or the driver?"

As you get dialed in with your self and who you really are, make that known when decisions are being made. You don't have to shout it. No need to whisper. Simply speak the truth about who you are. You'll be surprised at peoples' reactions when you come from this no-nonsense, gentle power.

If you do make the choice occasionally to give when you really don't want to, that giving will feel different to you. The giving won't feel dutiful. The end result may be exactly the same. But when you make a clear decision to give when you would rather not, it feels different. It's not automatic. It feels more like creating—and your heart will not shrink. You will sample the impact that choosing has on your spirit and yourself. Choosing and using your power in this way expands the self. It's an act of love.

Pay close attention to what happens inside as you start saying no or just think about saying no. This may give you some information about the benefit you get from saying yes. Let what you feel when you start to say no inform you. Notice who, where, and when saying no feels better and when it feels worse. Lastly, don't be surprised if you get a bit carried away with saying no. Think about a pendulum between the two extremes of always saying yes and always saying no. If you have more often than not said yes, when you start saying no, that pendulum may swing all the way to the other side before it finds a natural place somewhere in the middle.

One last thought before we conclude this chapter on anger. You've heard of the Type-A Personality and the Type-B Personality. The Type-C Personality is the Cancer Prone Personality. Research suggests that Type-C Personalities have a hard time paying attention to their own needs and saying no.[17]

Conclusion

Francie eventually befriended the anger she found inside. Once she had an internal reference for anger, she discovered it showing up in her life in lots of little ways—and some big ways, too. As she became skilled at acknowledging her own anger, she worked to accept it. And it was work. The anger scared and confused her. Feeling angry seemed foreign. She wanted to retract from this unfamiliar feeling. Since her external personality was fashioned as a woman who didn't get angry, accepting her anger was like rebuilding the self. But she kept accepting.

Eventually something curious happened. Her voice could be heard, literally and figuratively. Francie would come to session reporting instances when she found herself feeling angry during the previous week. More and more, she responded to those instances by expressing her disapproval. She said people would look at her funny, like, "Who is this?" But she liked respecting herself in this way. In time, relationships started to change. Her inner landscape was different. Her parents began treating her differently. She was beginning to reshape her life and she liked the shape of it.

The power held in her anger was emerging—not always perfectly, but it was emerging. Over the months, Francie became more and more effective with her power. Her life, as she said directly, felt better. Her life was teaching her that the more one operates in this kind of healthy power, the less one lives in anger, hurt, and fear. Conversely, the less one connects with healthy power, the more one lives in anger, hurt, and fear. Making contact with that wonderful, healthy power, lying in wait, often means going through the anger, hurt, and fear also waiting. Here's another opportunity to create the rest of your life. What will you make?

CHAPTER TWENTY-ONE

The Vehicle of Self

Defining the Self

We've talked a lot about the hardship road, the healing highway, and the self. But what exactly is the *Self*?

The Self is called many things: true self, higher self, God self, central sun, Brahman, Ptah, Buddha nature, Christ self, and by some, Holy Spirit or soul. Anita Moorjani, in her bestseller, *Dying To Be Me: My Journey From Cancer, To Near Death, To True Healing,* may provide us the best description of the Self: "In truth, I'm not my body, my race, religion, or other beliefs, and neither is anyone else. The real self is infinite and much more powerful...During my NDE [near death experience], there was nothing outside of my greater awareness because I was one with the entirety of Universal energy... The infinite self is our essence. It's who we truly are..."[18]

When I refer to the Self, I refer to us in our purest form and the purest form of ourselves is compassion. When I refer to *Source,* I intend to name that which is called many names by many cultures—most commonly, God. Source, for our purposes, is the original compassion-intentioned energy. So if Source is the origin of compassion, then as we grow in compassion, we become more like Source.

Each person brings his or her own name for Source, along with related beliefs, or the absence of beliefs, about Source. In the practice of psychotherapy for those finding their way through hardship, discussions about religion, faith, spirituality, or Source commonly arise.

Connecting With the Self

Here we're comparing the more limitless and expanded *Self* with the more limited and constricted *self*. Although it's difficult to talk about the self without reference to Source, the true focus of this chapter is the self. This may seem narcissistic. After all, great religions and contemporary thinkers suggest that we approach enlightenment when we get away from the self. But how can we get away from something we've never really had? How can we give our self away, as an act of love for others, if we don't love ourselves? How can we love ourselves if we don't know ourselves? How can we know ourselves if we don't attend to who we are?

The great band Genesis has a fitting refrain in their song, "Carpet Crawlers"[19]: "You got to get in to get out." You have to know yourself, which means essentially getting into yourself, before you can get out of, get away from, or give yourself.

Many have a weakened sense of self. Healing begins when we reconnect with our own wants and needs—when we *get into* our selves. Healing doesn't stop there, but this is where it often starts.

Connecting with yourself is an honest openness to what moves you to tears, scares the bejeebers out of you, rocks your world, ticks you off, pushes you away, awes you, touches a nerve, saddens you regularly, makes you laugh uncontrollably, etc.

A core message in the important book by Eckhart Tolle, *A New Earth*, is that the emotional pain many people feel is a result of the belief that they are not enough.[20] In other words, they're in pain because they believe they are not loveable. This same message is clearly reflected in the remarkable work by Cheri Huber, entitled *There Is Nothing Wrong with You: Going Beyond Self-Hate.*[21]

Compassion for ourselves helps us begin to believe we are enough, just the way we are. Compassion from others can help us stop trying to be and instead to simply be. Oddly enough, it is this simple state of just being that accelerates healing.

It's curious to watch what happens when the self begins to feel unconditionally loved. The self may get angry, feeling manipulated by this unconditional love; or become quiet, feeling unworthy; or feel scared, confused by this unfamiliar regard. In reaction to these feelings the self may become dominating or withdrawn or solicitous or manipulative. Many times the self simply leaves the person offering love.

However, if the self has the strength to stay, the unconditional love it receives frees it up to explore itself. In the presence of the raw power of this love, the self may stop trying to be what others think it should be.

This deep acceptance is a rich time in the development of the self, fueled first by love from someone or something else, then increasing fueled by the burgeoning love from within.

As the self begins to feel freed up inside because someone or something has loved it, it starts to discharge all kinds of feelings that have been lodged there—lodged inside because fear wouldn't let the self know those feelings. The feelings were too threatening or too big. In the safety of love, the self allows these feelings to be experienced. This new way of being with emotions begins to guide the self to the *Self.*

Practicing Self-Love

You may be thinking, "I've never known love like this." You may go so far as to think, "I never will." So then what? If you can begin to think more lovingly of yourself, there will be a quickening inside that feels good, and you'll want more of that. The self-love will help you grow. Then, thinking and feeling caringly about yourself will be easier the next time. You'll begin to get from within, what you may not have gotten from without.

Here's a little "how to" for getting self-love started. Every time you walk through a doorway ask, "What kind of thoughts am I having about me?" If you find recent thoughts about yourself sound like, "I shouldn't have said that to her," or, "When am I gonna have the guts to stop?" or, "What's my problem?" speak kindly to yourself instead. Simply develop a habit of noticing your thoughts, especially about yourself. If the thoughts don't love you, replace them with ones that do.

An indicator that you need self-love is when you notice you're having judgmental thoughts about others. We judge others as we judge ourselves.

The self, as it begins to love whomever it is when it's not trying so hard, starts the gradual and amazing process that gives birth to the *Self*. The Self is the one we truly are when we are not trying: the one we were born to be; the one most like Source, in a unique and magnificent way.

This birthing of the Self can be disorienting for the personality. Your habitual actions and thoughts that use to guide your way in the world have lost their charm. All the automatic reactions of the past are gone. Automatic has been replaced with authentic. That is, there's enough love for self to just show up. Period. That's a game changer.

The self, as it grows, tries on different thoughts, feelings, and behaviors. It's only through this process of trial and error that the self uncovers what is right for the Self. The emergence of the Self is a difficult time. Many folks during this transition regress because life may now feel too unfamiliar. That's OK. It is part of the process. As we continually extend compassion to the self when it takes these risks, it regains the strength required to come forward as the Self.

These forays can be tremendously exciting, though unnerving: "I'm gonna learn to Tango," "I told him something I've needed to get off my chest for years," "I bought a hot rod," "My wife and I did something in bed I never thought we'd do," "I got drunk for the first time," "I'm taking piano lessons." Now that it feels loved and is judging itself less, the self feels safe to venture out in these kinds of ways. Clinically, this state can be referred to as a more secure attachment with self.

In this developmental period toward the Self, religious and familial constraints often fall away. The self feels increasingly free and alive. The process of love begins to fuel itself. With new freedom, something quite interesting happens. Once the self feels really loved and ventures literally and figuratively to far and distant places, boundaries are reached: "Well, I got loaded again. Felt awful. Not sure I wanna get that wasted again." At this point the self is faced with choice—real choice—perhaps for the first time. In so doing, the self comes up against *its own* inner *parameters*—not those dictated by culture, religion or family. In making these choices, the Self steps forward.

Years ago, a Benedictine monastery served as my home for a short while. During a retreat for those of us who lived there, the abbot once shared, "Until you know that you have the potential to be a murderer, or a rapist, or an addict, you are more likely to become those things." Moving toward your Self is all about dancing with your shadow side. It's about exploring and embracing the parts of self that scare you the most.

When we have the courage to simply be, initially we may bump into parts of ourselves that make us really uncomfortable. When transformed, these parts are the very aspects that make us who we are. Until these most dreaded parts (often seen in our dreams) are engaged, they yank us around from the inside, in secret and in the shadows, seemingly beyond our control.

Once we venture toward those aspects of self that we fear and realize they are just parts, not all, we grow more comfortable with ourselves. This is the journey of integration and individuation.

Healing The Self Using Dreams

Often the parts of our dreams that terrify us most are the powerful parts of the self we have yet to accept. However, when we move toward these parts, by loving everything—EVERYTHING—about ourselves, we then begin to recover the power that those scary aspects of our dreams contain.

Many clients report dreams of being chased or cornered by some ominous and dangerous person or force. It's remarkable to hear these same clients develop command in their voices and actions as, over time, they take on the power locked in those dark dream characters. In Gestalt dream work, they might take on the persona of one of those terrifying demons or murderers and let it speak through them: "I am powerful beyond your wildest dreams. I could shred you before you even knew it!" The deep impact is palpable when the client is asked to repeat the first part of that statement, slowly: "*I...am... powerful...beyond...your...wildest...dreams.*"

Communicating from their shadowy aspect, I can almost see the client absorbing that character's strength. Over time using dream material in this way, the client repeatedly speaks with the power of the once terrorizing aspect. Eventually, an alliance is fashioned with these dark characters, integration begins, and the client walks taller, living and breathing the power once belonging to their shadow.

This is a path to self-love. It is a path of acknowledging and accepting everything that we are. As we take this journey, we appear more authentic. We impact our world. Others find us more interesting, and their love comes to us naturally. We feel that love. The true Self is sponsored.

The Outcome of Self-Love

The idea of self-love seems lost on many. Lots of clients make curious faces and say, "I really don't know what the heck you're talking about when you talk about me loving myself."

Many people, rather than loving the self, knowingly or not, battle the self. When we don't recognize this inner struggle, our energy is lost to it. In the end, the pain of that battle is turned on the self as shame, or on others as anger. The force of this dark energy expresses itself indirectly and often in ways that hurt others: sideways power.

When we learn to love ourselves completely from within and embrace even the most monstrous aspects of self (usually monstrous only by our own judgments) the power held by these dark aspects is transmuted into our own power, to be used as we see fit.

Eventually, how we see fit looks more and more like service to others. And not because it's "the highest good" or "right" or "the Christian thing to do." Love, including true self-love, by its nature becomes service. It spills over. We begin to see the Self. This is the deepest part of us, born and made of pure compassion.

The Self is confident, with no airs; powerful with no need to influence others; dramatically influential by simply being; healing to others, having deeply healed its self; loving and gentle with others from loving and being gentle with self; powerful, but not overpowering; caring deeply for others, but not at its own expense. This, then, is the Self.

CHAPTER TWENTY-TWO

Rest Stop #8: Move With– An Exercise in Resolution

Y ou've been in the car a long time together. If you're learning and practicing the art of saying no, things may be getting a bit tense in there, especially if the important people in your car—your life—are used to you saying yes. You can work this out without pulling off the recovery road and without giving away your power:

Move With–An Exercise in Resolution

Remember the show "Kung Fu?" Wouldn't miss it when I was a teen. Remember how the masters would stand nearly motionless while under attack, but opponents would fly? How can masters do this in real life?

Essentially, a master moves with, rather than against, the opponent. The master redirects the force brought by the opponent to neutralize that attacker.

For example, if an attacker rushes the master from the front, the master steps slightly aside while pushing the passing attacker lightly in the same direction the attacker is moving. This well placed and gentle push is enough to create imbalance in the attacker. The master stays relatively still. The attacker is put off-balance and then easily neutralized. The master does not attack back. That non-offensive tenet is central in many martial arts. It's not about winning. It's about neutralizing and then resolving without harm. Aggression is frowned upon and used only in the most extreme circumstances. A quiet mind is the master's weapon, and peace the victory.

You have probably already begun to make the translation from fistfights to verbal ones. When someone takes a verbal swing at you (criticizes you, minimizes you, won't listen, laughs at you, etc.), you may be inclined to play along or go off on that person: say yes or say no aggressively. Neither brings much resolution. There is a middle ground where you stand firmly, but don't get drawn into a shouting match.

During the hardship journey, especially if you've been traveling together with someone a long time, it is human to have relationship tension. Nerves get frayed and things get said. Here's an example of how that can go:

Verbal punch: "I can't believe you're still in bed. I know you're depressed, but come on."

Counterpunch: "Would you just get outta here. You don't have a clue what this is like."

Punch again: "Who needs a clue! Anybody could tell you're spending too much time in bed."

At this point, blood has been drawn. People have been hurt. So how can martial arts be applied to this kind of stressful communication? Sometimes move with your opponent.

Step 1. Put Your Ego in Your Pocket

The first step is the simplest of the three steps, but is by far the most important and the most difficult. When you put your ego in your pocket, you decide that loving is more important than winning. In reflecting this love, you don't counterpunch or apologize.

This may sound smaltzy, but the consequences of this simple decision can be profound. It doesn't mean, to be sure, that you should never speak up for yourself. Sometimes making yourself heard, getting angry, or saying no, even though others disagree or seem uncomfortable, is exactly what's needed. But other times, you may choose differently. This is the power and the liberation of choice.

The first step to moving with involves checking yourself. Putting your ego in your pocket can be very painful. Your pocket may not be big enough. Besides that, anything but fighting back may feel like giving in, not respecting the self, losing face, or giving power away. Often, the fear of losing power or some sense of mastery is what ongoing arguments are about. And, of course, these escalating arguments are more akin to talking to someone that's drunk—"fugeddaboudit." The real point gets lost in the emotion after tempers flare.

So, the first step in breaking this pain-producing cycle is for somebody to slowly back away from the need to win or control the other: ego in pocket. If this is a practice unfamiliar to you, it could feel like your relationship is going to cave in—scary. Don't expect the other person to get it right away. You've been sparring together this way for a long time: you punch, they punch; they punch, you punch. Be prepared for adjustment time. Putting your ego in your pocket is the relationship equivalent of the martial artist standing in potent stillness and not fighting back. This is power and mastery of another sort.

Step 2. Acknowledge What Was Said to You

When someone says "I can't believe you're still in bed. I know you're depressed, but come on," here's the move with part: "It's irritating for you to see me sleep so much." When attacked, the master gently redirects the attacker's force so as to neutralize. Move with.

Spouse drops mouth open. Why? Not from your punch, but precisely because this response isn't a counterpunch; isn't a comeback. This response instead channels the attacker's force and message, and flows with it. The "It's irritating for you . . ." statement acknowledges without agreeing. It *is not* saying, "You're right. I spend too much time in bed." It is saying, "I'm not interested in winning or fighting back. Nor am I interested in agreeing or conceding. I am interested in making this better and maybe even learning from it. And to start with, I want you to know I heard all of what you said." That's a lot.

The verbal, martial arts response acknowledges in one sentence what was said by the attacker. You, the attacked, simply do your best to rephrase the thoughts and feelings communicated by the attacker. You gather up the heart of the message sent your way, and with honest interest, you send a message back that says, "I get it." This way, your response moves *with* the attacker, rather than *against*.

You must have your ego in your pocket to do this. The nice thing is, if it works, the other person may start trying to communicate with you in the same way. The long-range result is you both feel heard more often. Sometimes that's enough.

Step 3. Ask for More Information

It helps to follow at this point with a question. So after responding to the verbal punch above with, "It's irritating for you to see me sleeping so much," you might add a question like, "What grates you about my sleeping?"

Now, if you're doing this for real, you might find that the other person responds to your lovely question with something like, "I'm frustrated! You don't do a thing around here." Well. Hmmm. Boy.

OK, so you now have another communication choice. You can take that ego back out of your pocket and attack as well: "And do know how many times I've said that to you?!" On the other hand, when the person counters with more attacking, it is possible to go with another round of Steps 2and 3: "Man, you are really steamed.

What has you so upset?" Presentation is everything. No sarcastic tones or nasty faces.

I was waiting one afternoon to meet with the leader of an organization. He supervised a large staff, and had asked me to systematically monitor each member of that group. When he arrived late for our appointment, he pointed to a chair in his office and literally said, "Sit!" Then he slammed the door so hard that pictures crashed to the floor. He then proceeded to launch a verbal assault on a report I had given him. While strongly tempted to counterpunch, I decided to instead use Steps 2 and 3 in some form or fashion.

Much as I wanted to go at him, my response instead flowed with his comment by reflecting back to him the issues he had with my report. Immediately he stopped dead in his tracks, explained the difficult situation he had just come from, and apologized for his behavior. It was then that he could actually hear me.

So, when attacked, you always have the punch back, block, duck and run options. More often than not, they just make things worse, and rarely resolve anything.

Or you can try this new stuff. For example, by changing up your response to the "You sleep too much" attack, the new and improved conversation might eventually reveal that your spouse is also completely exhausted. With that information, together you can fashion a way for both of you to get rested.

Alternately, it may become clear that your spouse really doesn't get your fatigue or its power over you. So, together you decide to talk about this with your family doctor. There are lots of possible responses at this point that could actually make things better.

But you have to be committed to improving the relationship. You have to choose a time to practice this technique when you have the necessary strength. Of course, you can go about business as usual. It's yours to decide.

CHAPTER TWENTY-THREE

Driving Alone: Changes in Your Support System

You've logged many hours on the hardship highway with those you love. Things are getting better. The crisis is over. The focus that came early on—the newness—is long past. But the return to a more routine life may be lulling everyone to sleep.

Sooner or later, the people supporting you and your family may begin to nod off one by one. They were there through the tough times. You are very glad for that. But what happened to everybody? Where'd they all go? The greeting cards have stopped. The phone calls aren't as often. No more casseroles in the fridge. While one part of you is glad, some other part may feel something different.

You might start to feel alone with your tragedy, and you're not sure you're ready for that. If you are the support person or the helping professional, you too may start to feel you're carrying the weight by yourself.

For the survivor, a spouse or best friend is usually the last to nod off. Just like on long drives, they want to stay awake with you, but eventually even those closest slip into sleep. They don't mean to.

Unfortunately, some of your supporters may just feel that they can't give anymore. They're emotionally spent. They need rest. They may feel they have gotten as close as they can. They may have their own hardship and family issues. So you're alone at the wheel.

You can always jostle those nearest, and let them know you still want their support. On the other hand, solitude has its own power. If you can find that power, driving with everyone else asleep is much more doable. There are some very useful techniques out there designed to help you find power in solitude. Many of these approaches guide you through an inner journey, using your mind and active imagination, such as those mentioned in Chapter 5. You'll find resources that offer some of these tools listed in the bibliography.

It's important to acknowledge—as a survivor attending a presentation pointed out to me—not everyone dealing with hardship has a travel companion. If you are one of those survivors who has been on the journey alone, your road has perhaps been especially trying. Consider finding support groups on-line or in your community.

If you've had support all along your hardship journey, the solitude may be exactly what you need right now. It's OK. After the quiet time—the time taken to be with your own spirit, thoughts, and feelings—the road will still be there. This isn't a race. It's a journey.

CHAPTER TWENTY-FOUR

Rest Stop #9: Sleep and the Racing Mind

Why is it that nodding off behind the wheel seems so dang easy, but falling asleep on your own pillow sometimes seems impossible? It has to do with your brain wave activity. If you have difficult falling asleep a simple exercise that capitalizes on brain function can help you fall asleep more quickly.

Anxiety is one of the most common emotions experienced during the journey beyond hardship. Generally, anxiety is considered a fear-based response. Although fear, like so many difficult emotions, is often thought of as negative, like all emotions, it is intended to inform us. At its simplest level, fear protects us. Without fear, all of us would constantly be injured, physically and emotionally.

Fear, like a car alarm tells us when something is not right. Thank goodness for this warning system. However, significant anxiety is like the too-sensitive car alarm. It goes off unnecessarily, eventually becoming a nuisance rather than an aid. For a lot of survivors and support people who are trying to fall asleep, the racing, anxious mind is like the sensitive car alarm that just keeps going off, making it impossible to rest. What's this about, and why is it so much easier to get drowsy behind the wheel?

The racing mind, like the sensitive car alarm, is just doing its job. It's simply doing it too well. Mental activity is often an attempt to create firm ground on which to stand. During times of hardship so much happens and changes. Nothing seems stable. By constantly turning thoughts, situations, and experiences over and over in the mind, the mind is trying to order an otherwise chaotic-feeling circumstance. This organizing function comforts us and helps us live more productively.

But when the mind won't stop organizing, grinding, and racing, something very uncomfortable and unproductive occurs, particularly when trying to sleep. The racing mind becomes too much of a good thing. With a habitually racing mind, the process of constantly organizing your thoughts has become a kind of addiction—an attempt to make you feel better that actually harms you in the long run. So, like managing withdrawal for the addict, it's not a matter of stopping the mind from activity all together, but stepping it down gradually to a lesser rate.

Stepping down brain activity is what happens on the highway without even trying, and why it can be difficult *not* to fall asleep while driving. Your mind may be going a mile a minute when you start the drive, but it gradually busies itself, especially at night, on the passing signs, white lines and posts. Unconsciously, the mind begins to let go of racing thoughts as it shifts into watching the environment. This simple mental focus that happens automatically on the highway is the basis for most meditation techniques. The mind is continuing to be active, but in a much simpler way, and brain wave activity changes and slows.

Did you know that Einstein's theory of relativity came to him in his sleep? How many times have you woken up with a solution to a problem? Have you also noticed that many solutions seem to just pop into your mind, when you're doing something besides thinking about "the problem?" This is good reason to let your mind relax, especially when trying to sleep.

It appears that a racing mind just recycles the same information, over and over. With so much activity, there's rarely room for any new information to surface. Yet, when we sleep or focus on other things, the information related to a problem settles and even reconfigures itself, leading to new ideas and the emergence of something completely different. This is the creative process, and an effective approach to problem solving.

The point here is that a running, non-stop mind does very little to help fix the perceived problem. Instead, try the following exercise when attempting to fall asleep. It gives the mind something else to focus on, like passing highway lines do. And who knows? With the mind quiet, some real and useable information might surface that actually helps with a problem.

Sleep and the Racing Mind

Read all of the steps. When you're finished, you can record the suggested script and replay it when it's time to sleep. Or, have someone else read the script to you as you fall asleep.

Step 1. Breathe and Be Gentle with Your Mind

A racing mind indicates anxiety, which is a fear-based response to life. Fear-based responses are designed to protect you. As such, fear-based responses actually gear you up. To do that, fear-based responses release chemicals in the body that ready it to fight or run. So could this be any more contrary to what you want when you lie down to sleep? Have you ever noticed when trying to fall asleep that after a while of the mind racing, you just feel like getting up and doing something? That's exactly what the chemicals released in the body during a fear-based response are designed to do—initiate action.

The body's call to action is generally accompanied by rapid and shallow breathing. The shallow breath supports the body's release of action-oriented chemicals. The more chemicals that are released, the more shallow the breath, and the more shallow the breath, the more chemicals are released, and so on. That's when you jump out of bed. Sleep, you know at this point, is impossible.

Three ingredients are key in this buildup to action. There's the *mind racing* to create a sense of order during a time in your life that feels chaotic. There's *shallow breathing*. Finally, there's the *release of action-oriented* chemicals in the body. Believe it or not, you have the capacity to address all three of these ingredients. By consciously shifting the racing mind and the breath, you can alter the body's release of action-oriented chemicals. Start by shifting the breath.

The first part of Step 1 is simply to breathe. When you become conscious of your breath and begin to slow it down by breathing deep, full breaths, you are sending a message to your body that says, "It's OK. At this moment, things are all right."

If you do nothing else but take deep, full breaths, you will begin to change your body chemistry. Your body will begin to feel, "It's OK to just lie here. Fighting or running is not required right now." If your breath has been shallow, your body thinks it's preparing for action. Changing your breath can change the quality of your thoughts, and your chemistry.

Now that you've slowed your breathing, be gentle with your mind. If your mind tends to race, that habit isn't going to stop overnight. You've been operating in the world that way for years. So, be patient as you try some other way. Remember, when your mind races, it's trying to help you. Your mind wants to create the feeling of mastery over the troubling situation.

So as you move into Steps 2 and 3, your mind may have a tendency to get off course and start to race again. That's OK. Gently invite your mind to return to the thoughts suggested in the next step. If it helps, speak with your mind: "I know you want to help me by racing to solution, mulling over the situation again and again. But when you race, my body gets charged up, and I find it difficult to settle down. I want to settle down. I trust that any improvements I might make in my situation will become clear to me, even if I stop thinking about them right now. So thank you for trying to help, but what I want and need is to return my mind to the thoughts suggested by this exercise."

Why is it important to be gentle with your mind? If you start getting frustrated with the fact that in the middle of this exercise your mind wants to race again, you might set up a win-lose situation inside your own head. It can happen when you turn this exercise into a task you must successfully complete. When that happens, you may begin to speak to your mind with demands like, "You will stop racing. I will go to sleep." Most of us tend to resist demands, even when they come from some part of ourselves.

At this point, it's as if one part is saying, "You will sleep," and another part responds with, "I don't think so," or, "You can't make me." Then you're stuck. You can avoid this win-lose by not demanding that your mind perform but by inviting it to slow down. Not only that, if you demand that your mind slow down, and your mind has trouble satisfying that demand (because going slow has not been your mind's norm), then you might become anxious, which fuels the release of those fear-based, action-oriented chemicals. Now you're up again.

As an aside, if you do nothing more than call up the _feeling_ of being loved, and rest in that, you might fall asleep.

Step 2. Return to Your Body

The human body carries an electrical charge. It's this charge that fires across nerve endings and gives rhythm to the heart muscle.

That's why medical professionals use paddles that send electricity to the heart when it stops.

Science tells us that whenever an object carries an electrical charge, there is an electromagnetic field in and around that object. Because the human body does carry an electrical charge, there is then an electromagnetic field in and around it. This field, which may be stronger in some, has been depicted in art for thousands of years, often as a halo or radiance around the body of mystics, masters, and saints. Many cultures over the centuries have developed ways to work with this field for the purposes of health. Today, the National Institute of Health is studying contemporary techniques employed by medical professionals who balance and strengthen this electromagnetic or bioenergetic field in and around humans to support wellness, happiness, and wholeness.

Interestingly enough, an organization called The HeartMath Institute has instrumentation capable of not only measuring the bioenergetic field in humans, but the frequency and strength of that field in and around each major organ. According to their research, the strength of the bioenergetic field of the heart is 5000 times greater than that of the brain![22] How many pictures and statues of saints and gods in multiple religions show rays coming from the heart?

It appears the human electromagnetic field is egg-shaped, with the larger end around the shoulders and head, and the smaller end at the feet. Consider that when your mind is racing, there's a lot of electricity firing in and around your head. Consider that as the mind races, more and more electricity is sent to your head, expanding the electromagnetic field there while draining it from the rest of your body. Have you ever felt empty and cold when your mind is racing? Have your legs felt weak? "I just didn't feel like I had my legs under me."

Step 2 suggests that you return to your body. That is, imagine that your electromagnetic field is gently pouring back into the rest of your body from the area around your head. Here's a visualization to help. This visualization gives your mind something to chew on, like the white lines on the highway, as a sort of racing-mind step-down program.

If you like, after you've slowed your breathing as suggested in Step 1, read the following paragraphs to yourself, or have someone read it to you, or record it and play it back when you're ready to sleep. Remember to be kind with your mind if it wants to race as you read or listen:

My mind is racing to support me, but at this point I'd like to settle down and fall asleep. To help me fall asleep, I am taking deep, full breaths. And as my mind and my breath slow down, I am occupying my mind with this image: I see my electromagnetic field like a very large soap bubble attached to the top of my head. With each slow inhale, I see the bubble shrinking, as if my inhale is drawing air into my body from inside the bubble.

As this air from inside the bubble is drawn down through the top of my head, it is converted into a beautiful gold light, like honey. And as I continue to breathe, this honey-like light begins to make its way into every cell of my body, bringing calm and quiet.

First, the honey-like light slowly fills my head, my neck, and my shoulders. As it fills these areas, I feel them relax. Next, the honey drains into my upper arms, then my lower arms and now my hands. And as the light reaches these areas, they relax as if each and every cell is filling with pure love.

Now the honey-like light makes its way into the cells of my upper back and chest, and as it does, I actually feel the muscles there relaxing, receiving the love of this light.

As I breathe in deeply, the bubble above my head gets smaller, and the honey-like light now drains into my middle back and my belly. It feels comforting. As this honey-light pours through me, there is a release of tension as each area is filled and relaxed.

With each deep breath, the golden light makes its way farther down my body, now pouring comfortably into my lower back, my hips, and my groin region. I am finding myself more and more quiet inside as I watch the golden light move through me.

Now the light is in my upper legs and then my knees, and the golden light is filling the cells in my legs with calm and love, and I enjoy the relaxation. And the honey-light continues to pour down into my shins and calf muscles. And now I see that the bubble above my head is nearly completely gone, as each inhale has emptied it, and the activity contained there has been converted into a golden light, like honey, now reaching my ankles and, finally, filling me completely. The sensation I'm left with is one of fullness, relaxation, and pure love.

Step 3. Plant Yourself

Native Americans believe that all things have a principal essence or spirit. The earth, for example, has an essence more like the beat of the heart, slow and rhythmic, like the movement of the turtle, paced, predictable, and deliberate, like the color of the soil, dark and rich, and like the sound of the horse walking.

The essence of the sky is more like the firing of nerve endings, like lightning, quick and erratic, like the flight of the hummingbird, excited, charged and changing, like the color of clouds, light and airy, and like the sound of the wind.

As people, we also each have a principal essence. Some of us tend to be more earth-like; others, more sky-like. One is no better than the other. Both bring unique gifts. Earth people are solid folks. You know exactly where they stand. They are more like the buffalo. Sky people are a joy to be around. They accomplish much. They are more like the fox or the bird.

Nature demonstrates daily the value of balance in all things. Balance between earth and sky brings life. We see this in the cycles of the seasons: rain to nourish, sun to flourish, wind to prune, and cold to transition into new life. Disasters caused by too much sky or rain make the consequences of imbalance painfully apparent. On the other hand, drought is an example of not enough sky.

Balance between earth essence and sky essence in people also brings life. For example, a person with healthy balance between the essence of earth and sky can be solid in beliefs, but open; can be very productive, and still know peace.

People with too much earth essence may wish to be more motivated and sometimes feel stuck. On the other hand, people with too much sky essence often wish they could just relax.

I used to be very much a sky person. My movements were fast, my speech was fast, my stomach was fast, and my mind was always active. My mind and my body used to move a lot when trying to sleep. With time and support, I have found a balance that serves me better. As a result, my movements have slowed, my speech is deeper and more deliberate, my stomach rests, and my mind can be still. Sleep comes easier.

Given these notions, if you regularly have trouble falling or staying asleep, you may have too much sky essence and not enough earth essence. To increase your earth essence, consider now adding the following visualization to those already suggested above, and Plant Yourself:

My body feels full and weighty. The honey-like light has filled me in from top to bottom. The fullness I feel is comforting. I feel loved.

The honey-like light I feel in every cell of my body is now beginning to gather in my feet. Because of this, I feel a subtle pressure in my arches, as this light of love pushes against them from the inside out.

Finally, the weight of the honey-like light pooling in my legs and feet is so present that the bottoms of my feet open, allowing the light to gently ooze out.

I continue to feel great peace, fullness, and love in every cell of my body, as the honey-like light pours gently from the bottoms of my feet, making its way past my bed, through my home to the earth below. As this honey-like light reaches the earth, it begins to turn a darker color, like molasses or deep, rose-petal red. And as it reaches the earth and turns this darker color, it begins to stretch into the earth, like roots.

These dark roots coming from the bottoms of my feet are reaching deep into the soil. As these roots stretch into the earth, I feel an even greater sense of calm, as if any tension or unwanted activity of mind or body is being pulled down, through my body, and out the bottoms of my feet.

These dark roots continue to stretch farther and farther into the heart of the earth, and as they do, I feel a profound sense of trust, like a tree firmly planted and completely stable. I feel this from the top of my head to the very bottoms of my feet.

And like a tree firmly planted, as the dark roots reach farther into the rich soil of the earth, these same roots begin to nourish me, bringing back to me an even richer sense of love, health, and calm. As these nourishing feelings return to me from the earth, my body responds with pure stillness, relaxation, peace, and comfort. I am finding it easy to begin to slip into a state of rich restfulness.

Sleep is now upon me. I am full from head to toe and in every cell of my body with a sense of profound calm, experiencing deep love in all of me. And the earth is sending even more quiet and compassion into me through the bottoms of my feet. Sleep is here. I am one with all that is at rest.

CHAPTER TWENTY-FIVE

Rest Stop #10: The Road Map of Dreams

Most of us, at one time or another, have gotten lost while driving. It's no different with the journey beyond hardship. Interestingly, your dreams may be the best map back to who you really are. I wrote my master's thesis on dreams and have worked with dreams for more than 35 years. Dream work is an integral part of my counseling practice. Dreams may tell you more about yourself than any other experience. Even though you may be dreaming about others, it's all about you.

The experience of dreaming cannot be explained or contained in any one theory or even cultural stance. Though the approach that has proven most useful to me is the Gestalt model, I value and sometimes introduce other avenues for understanding dreams.

For example, God, insight, spirit, angels, and all sorts of other holy things have been reported by many cultures over the centuries to show up in dreams. In the Torah and the New Testament there are numerous stories about the presence of God and other spiritual influences in dreams. These texts represent only two of the great religions. No single dream approach neatly contains all this, so some openness to all dream theories makes sense.

Gestalt psychotherapy says we all have an instinct for wholeness, which shows up most clearly in dreams. Many consider such an instinct sacred. This may sound odd since so many dreams seem anything but whole or sacred.

When you look at the gestalt of a dream, which means the whole or total image, the idea of sacred makes more sense. Take for example the dream of being chased by a bad person. In the Gestalt approach, both the one chasing and the one being chased are aspects of the person dreaming. Most people who experience this sort of dream discover through working with the image that some important part of them is being opposed by another important part of them. One goal of Gestalt therapy is to minimize these kinds of polarities. When that happens, some integration has begun—steps to greater degrees of wholeness. When experienced, this can feel sacred.

If a client brings a dream to therapy, his or her interpretation is always the most important place to start. If someone brings a dream and says their dream is an answer to prayer, then I accept it to be that. If a client brings a dream and says, "This dream is about my relationship with my father," then it is true. If someone brings a dream and says, "My sister who died four months ago visited me in my dream last night," then I accept it to be so. If a person brings a dream and says, "This dream was so real. Almost like it was more than a dream. I keep having it. I wonder if it's past life stuff," then we would explore it together with that possible understanding.

Maybe one of these shared ideas is all the client needs and the dream work ends there. But if the client is interested, we can look behind or under or around the initial understanding to see if more information may be stored in the dream.

A way into this expanded discussion of the dream comes from how the client tells the dream. If he or she repeatedly speaks about a character or image from the dream, that particular character or image probably holds key information. The same goes if the client changes facial or body expressions or tone of voice when talking about a particular part of a dream.

It usually works best if the client tells the dream as if it were happening right now: "I am running," rather than, "I was running." In this way, the dream becomes more an experience and less a report.

Let's imagine that I have a client named Tom. What follows is Tom's presentation of a dream: "This is a strange dream. I'm walking through the attic of this old house. I think it's the house I grew up in. I really liked that house, but I didn't like the attic, so it's weird that I'm in that part of the house." He then pauses and looks up, slightly pained. Two or three seconds later he gets a little smile and says, "I had such fun times with my brothers and sisters in that house. We used to chase each other all over the yard. . . . Anyway, I'm a little spooked about being in the attic. Not as bad as I was as a kid, but a little skittish. This is where it gets strange. All of a sudden, this trap door opens in front of me and I just miss falling through it." At this point Tom's eyes widen: "Scared the dickens outta me. I think I woke up right after that. I was kind of shaking."

If Tom offered no interpretation of the dream, I might begin a Gestalt exercise like this: "OK. So let's take a look. What would you say are the central parts or symbols of this dream?" Tom thinks for a second and then lists the house, and the attic, the trapdoor, and him. My follow-up question is, "So, of these pieces, which is the most important to you?" Tom says the trapdoor is the most important piece of the dream.

With that, we begin: "Tom, I'm gonna ask you to role-play a little with me, and it'll probably feel a bit strange at first. No worries. Try not to work to hard at it. Just let it happen. This is your dream and your experience. I'll follow you. FYI, in the Gestalt approach, it's less about interpreting the dream and more about the dream speaking for itself. One way to find out what the dream has to say is to let each part have a voice."

"The play-acting we're about to try is designed to do just that. Ready to give it a try? OK, as odd as this might seem, I want to speak with you, as the trapdoor. What I'd like you to do is move to someplace else in the room where you think the trapdoor might show up. Once you're in that new place, I'm going to have a conversation with you as the trapdoor."

Tom has decided to stand in the center of the office, like a trapdoor in my floor. When Tom gives the trapdoor its own voice in this new position, he is more comfortable letting that symbol speak for itself, as if that symbol is some separate person. As a result, Trapdoor's words come more freely—less filtered—and therefore more authentic and believable.

I say to Tom, "Now in this place, you are the trapdoor. I want you to talk in first person as if you, a trapdoor, can speak. As if you, trapdoor, have a voice…Trapdoor, what should I call you?"

Tom hesitates briefly, blinks a few times and then says casually, "My name is 'No Good.'"

So we begin our dialogue: "No Good, as a place to start, please describe yourself to me."

"I'm about this big, and on the floor of the attic, but I'm filled with darkness,"

"No Good, would you say that again please?" I ask.

"I'm about this big, and on the floor of the attic, but I'm filled with darkness."

I then say, "Would you repeat just that last part, No Good?"

"But I'm filled with darkness."

"No Good, can you share more with me about your darkness?"

"The darkness . . .," Tom starts.

I interject, "My darkness . . ."

"OK, *my* darkness is very thick. I scare people because of it, just like I scared Tom in the dream. People are afraid to get close to me because of my darkness."

"No Good, say that last sentence again," I request.

"People are afraid to get close to me because of my darkness." At this point, Tom tears up—something has begun to move in him.

So, that would be our initiation into this dream. Then, I gently invite Tom back to his chair to explore the surfacing emotion. Later in that same session, I might have Tom himself talk to No Good. Or

I might invite Tom to move to yet another place in the office and dialogue with me as if he were No Good's darkness.

By giving voice to each of these aspects of the dream, Tom becomes more familiar with these parts of himself. As parts become known, they become less threatening. Eventually, parts that were tremendously opposed start to actually have a conversation. This may take time, and repeated sessions, but eventually the dreamer reflects more calm and strength overall.

The process unfolds itself in this way, led by the cues the client gives. As you see, this approach is not about "interpretation"; it's about letting the dream and all its players speak for themselves.

You might say, "Well, Tom was just making all that stuff up as the trapdoor." You would be exactly correct. If we gave the same setup to five different people and asked each of them to become the trapdoor, we would have five very different responses, beginning with the name they might choose for the trapdoor.

As a result, the dream characters and all they share are about the dreamer and nobody else. The pieces come together very quickly and often with much emotion. Doors open to understanding. With understanding comes a stronger sense of choice. And while sometimes opening us to a degree of internal strife, the outcome often means a fuller sense of self, and more life.

Here's a Nine-Step approach for using these concepts to work with your own dreams:

The Road Map of Dreams

Step 1. Identify the part of your dream most important to you—probably the part that comes to mind quickly or the part you feel strongest about, either positively or negatively.

Step 2. Identify the significant "character" from this important part of your dream. This character can be a person, an object, an animal, or even a feeling or sound.

Step 3. Give this character a name. If the character has a real name like Nancy or Spot, you can use that name or you can use a name that more closely fits what you felt in the dream about that character. Let this name come from your gut, not your mind, e.g., Ugly Creature or Angel Voice. Use any name that speaks to you—Brave, Broken Down Car, White Horse, Confused, Carousel, Vast, or Precious Child, etc.

Step 4. Fold a piece of paper in half and write your name at the top of one column and your character's name at the top of the other column.

Step 5. Write a script between you and your dream character, listing responses under the appropriate name on your divided page. A good place to start is for you to write this statement to your character: "Describe yourself to me." For example, if your character's name is

Broken Down Car, it might respond to your opening statement with something like, "I'm big, but I'm kind of a wreck. There are holes in me." And you might respond with, "What happened to you?" Write all this down in the columns. Let the dialogue continue freely and without filtering until it feels finished. Be sure that each of you responds only in first person, i.e., "*I'm* kind of a wreck," not, "*It's* kind of a wreck."

Step 6. If something uncomfortable happened in your dream that you're still uneasy about, this step is useful. Find some time to be quiet and go back into the dream. See the dream as if it was happening right now, but use your power to recreate the uncomfortable dream experience in a way that supports you or makes you feel better, i.e., you outrun or overpower your attacker; you sprout wings and fly before you hit the ground. Try not to get stuck within these recreations. Do what comes naturally, and if you struggle to resolve the situation, breathe compassion into yourself, and try again later. These are only images intending to teach you.

Step 7. Put your dialogue aside for a few days; a week or more is OK. This distance created by time helps shake any literal translation you might still hold to. Then *read only the words under your dream character's name*. As you read these words, they should be in first person, like, "I'm a white, powerful horse. I am strong and full of life," or, "I am only two years old, and because I have no legs, I can't stand on my own." Read those words again, out loud.

Step 8. Write down any of your reactions once you've read your character's words out loud.

Step 9. Consider these questions: Does this dream have anything to say to you? Do the words from your character remind you of any part of you? Does the feeling you have when reading your character's words resemble the feeling of any part of your life today? How might this information impact how you choose to be in the future?

You may find these nine steps useful in tapping a truly powerful resource. The wisdom, guidance, and truth offered by your dream life can be potent and healing. This built-in therapy is available every night for free. This map guides you to your true Self and to greater wholeness.

Chapter Twenty-Six

Nearing Your Destination: Signs You're Getting Close

Is feeling more whole the goal of your journey beyond hardship? What about a quiet mind? How about health and joy? Or do you seek improved relationships? Perhaps you're after parts of all these intentions. What is your journey's destination? It's different for everyone, and like any long trip, you'll see signs when you're getting close.

As you approach your destination, you may notice more happiness in your heart or more trust in your relationships. You might discover that your attention is returning to the rest of life—the parts that were background earlier in the hardship journey are now more foreground. You may find that the first thing you think about in the morning is not your tragedy. You may notice that sounds or sights or smells related to your trauma don't stir you up like they use to. You might realize a freshness in your spirit. Your actions may show that you value something today that is different from what you valued this time last year.

Excellent. You're on your way. Often, life feels more satisfying once we have passed through the most difficult part of the hardship. You deserve every second of your renewed sense of well-being.

But may I offer a note of caution. As a culture, we tend to judge just about everything including who had the best trip. If you're finding holes in your journey, or think you should feel better than you do, or focus on a part of your life that you've decided just isn't up to par, please consider simply accepting your journey as it unfolds.

What if there was no "best destination"—just the one you hoped for and wanted? What if you traveled toward that destination with trust? What if in traveling with trust, your hopes and wants gently changed and developed along the way? What if you found this way of traveling gratifying?

Have you ever just taken off in your car, not knowing where you were going? What a fascinating way to head out on a Saturday morning. One weekend, I pulled into a gas station and saw several couples on motorcycles. I asked where they were headed. They replied, "We don't know. We'll find out when we get there."

This kind of travel can be extra relaxing. In those glorious hours, something lovely happens. It's just about being. In just being, every goal for that drive is satisfied. What an interesting way to live. It's the difference between living in trust and living in fear. It's not about being lazy or not having plans. In a state of trust more is usually accomplished because actions born from love and trust are in line with natural passions and energies.

There's a little waterfall fountain in my office. I'll joke with clients that the water doesn't gather at the top and ask, "Well guys, what's the best way down?" And sometimes I'll pull a small stone from the base and stick it in the middle of the flow: "OK, now we need a committee to figure the greenest and most efficient route around the stone." The water's destination with the added stone remains unchanged, and even as I place the stone, the water has modified its course: effortless. And no less is being accomplished. Our destinations may be very similar, but the spirit with which we travel can make the journey itself quite different.

It's been my privilege to lead thousands of support group meetings for hundreds of men and women surviving hardship. My ears have heard many stirring stories, thoughts, and feelings in these most honorable exchanges. My eyes have witnessed courage in the face of pain of every kind: body, mind, and spirit. People in these groups wrestled with torments of every sort. Over the months and years, individuals and entire groups painstakingly peeled through layers of human values.

Many hardship survivors peeled away the value of needing power over others. Some pulled away from the value of prestige. Some dug through the layers of value associated with wealth and possessions. Beneath those, some ventured past layers of friendships that really weren't. Even the value of family and faith as they knew them were explored. Finally, health, hope, pain and life itself were all scrutinized, analyzed, and peeled away because hardship opened these matters for deeper consideration. The one thing that remained, the one value that stuck, the one destination most often sought by travelers on the journey beyond hardship was love—to love and be loved.

Chapter Twenty-Seven

Ongoing Survivorship: The Worst Is Over But The Journey Isn't

When the devastation and pain typical of the start of a hardship journey eases, the road seems smoother. Somehow you've managed to move yourself down the road a piece, and you're actually doing pretty well. It's a good time to park it in the garage and enjoy the better life you've created. But life by its nature doesn't end there. Whether or not life brings more difficult times in the years to come, the hardship just survived can provide the necessary ingredients for the continued development of the *Self*. So some survivors keep driving.

This kind of ongoing travel may be difficult to comprehend.

A younger woman got her support group's attention one night with these thoughts: "In just a few weeks, it's gonna be a year since I got outta jail. I'm doing really well, and I'm thankful every day. But I still need to come to this meeting once a month."

"'Still need?'" I said. "That suggests that at some point you shouldn't need."

"Well," she shared, "it helps to be around you all, but my husband doesn't always get it."

"What tells you that?" I asked.

"When I was getting ready to come tonight he asked me where I was going, and when I told him, he just kind of walked away from me. I asked him what was wrong and he said, 'I don't know. I guess I don't understand why you still need that group.'" She got quiet.

"What effect do those kinds of comments from your husband have on you?" I asked.

Though it was hard for her to speak, words made their way out: "Sometimes I feel alone in my own house."

To be sure, many people are very happy to forget the entire hardship experience. For others, there is a continuing concern it will never be forgotten. Then there are those who never want to forget because of all that the tragedy taught. They intentionally remember it, so as to maintain new ways of life that serve them better.

Many who believed they would never be free of "hardship thoughts" find they can go a long time without them. And there are actually survivors who completely forget.

But, then there are times it can be difficult to think of anything but the tragedy: times of year, seasons, anniversaries, birthdays. These moments in the continuing journey can be especially disturbing. There may be emotion waves when returning to the scene of the tragedy, even years later. You might call these *occasion reactions*. If someone is having one of these occasion reactions, it only makes things worse when others say, "Why are you still getting upset about this?"

These occasion reactions provide a perfect opportunity for practicing self-care and effective communication. If you are the one having the occasion reaction, but not feeling supported, acknowledge what you feel. You have a right to ask for what you need. Teach your support person to ask you who, what, where, when, and how questions as pain like this shows up: "How are you doing being back in your old neighborhood?" or, "What effect is this trip to the lawyer having on you?" In teaching others these skills, you are being responsible for yourselves.

If you're supporting someone having an occasion reaction, listen with your heart and question with love. Simply be present, not to resolve but to learn. Ask questions in an authentic, open way, without accusation. Ask those open-ended questions, and then practice the simple but powerful art of golden silence. Try not to turn your questioning into an interrogation or a lesson on how to get over the pain. If you see patterns in your survivor's answers, share them if you think it will help.

If you haven't been through what the person having the occasion reaction has been through, you probably don't understand. If you haven't been the primary support person to someone dealing with true hardship, you probably don't understand. As tough as it may be to comprehend, the survivor or support person you love may need help with the pain of hardship for years to come. It can be an opportunity for both of you to gain knowledge of one another, thereby deepening the intimacy you share. The journey continues.

CHAPTER TWENTY-EIGHT

Beyond the Mountaintops: The Journey of Death and Dying

For some facing hardship, the human journey ends. And for some, that end comes swiftly. For others, their bodies decline steadily. To those survivors whose bodies are in decline, respect this part of your journey as you have all others and ask those supporting you to do the same. You may decide to stay in some form of medical care, even until death. This is an honorable choice. Or there may come a time when you choose to discontinue some or all of your medical care. This, also, is an honorable choice. Know that whatever you decide is exactly the right thing for you.

If you can, make decisions about how you want to die (e.g., when or if to use life support, etc.) while your mind is still clear and capable. If you worry that you won't be able to tell when your mind is failing, let your family or someone you strongly trust know that you are worried. Then ask them to tell you when they see the very early signs of your mind weakening. This way, you will know it's time to address big decisions, if you haven't already.

Whatever you decide, some will support your choices and some will not. If you decide to continue medical care or treatment until death, some will say, "You shouldn't put yourself through that," or "Why are you still holding on? Why can't you just let go?" Remember, it is your journey, not theirs.

If you decide to discontinue part or all of your medical care or treatment, some will say, "You shouldn't give up. There's still hope," or, "My illness is worse than yours. I would give anything to be in your shoes. And you want to stop treatment? That's not fair." But it's your journey, not theirs.

Choosing to stop some medical care or treatment is just that—a choice. It's not necessarily giving up. It may be a solid, well thought-out and determined decision. It may simply be, in your mind, the best choice, all things considered. This choice may scare folks around you. It may force them to look more closely at the reality of the situation. For some, your choice may make them think about an option they are not quite ready to consider. Their uncomfortableness may come out as anger. But the choice is still yours.

Giving up is also a choice. But giving up has such a negative connotation. Maybe we should call it giving in. Or surrendering. Or simply *giving*. That may say it best for some people—giving peace to one's own heart and the hearts and spirits of those who love you.

Twilight

Twilight is that time between stages of light at day's end that changes the way things look. During the twilight of life, things start to look and feel different. Twilight during the hardship journey happens when dying becomes more imminent. Twilight occurs in a few ways. This time between life and death can begin subtly, as the survivor contends with mental, emotional, and/or physical complications or recurrences. Of course, complications and recurrences don't automatically mean the survivor is on a sure path to death. During these times, the survivor and those supporting the survivor may have fleeting thoughts about the possibility of death. This can be an unusual period of continued hope and quiet grieving.

The other occasion of twilight is when the survivor is more definitely approaching death. This is the time when all recognize that the survivor is probably going to die. The transition from more hope to less hope ensues. The shift from less grief to more grief unfolds.

Curious behaviors may surface in family and friends. Some involved with the dying survivor may begin to race about trying to stop the sun from setting. That is, trying to halt what is inevitable—the death of the one they love. This can be unsettling as these people hold fiercely to tiny bits of hope. That's how the love is often expressed in those last moments of light, feverishly searching the Internet for potential cures and last-ditch-effort approaches—and bellies full of pain. But the sun continues to set.

In time, though, often following the lead of the person dying, one by one those who love him or her surrender to their own longings for hope and ease their wrestling with the sun. Acceptance is dawning. At this point, waves of hurt overtake many. One person is affected, and then feels better for a time. Then another person feels the waves crash. Families can get confused by this rhythm of pain.

Someone may be hurting in the morning, but much better later that same day. Or someone else will be all right, but that person's spouse is struggling. It might begin to feel like roulette, never knowing who's going to be OK and who's not.

Some support people try to change themselves with each new set of circumstances and emotions. Whether you're loved one died suddenly or is dying slowly, be only who you are. The journey is long, and the toughest roads are just ahead. When you find something pleasant, enjoy it. At a time like this, the spirit absolutely needs refreshment. It can feel like you're expected to be in constant pain when someone you love has died or is dying. If you are in constant pain, so be it. However it's not a requirement when grieving. Be assured that if you are an honest human being, you will have genuine pain. And some times you may feel it. Others times, not.

Follow the dying person's lead. If he or she wants to talk, then listen without saying "It's gonna be OK" or "Don't talk like that." If the dying person wants to go on with life as best he or she can, try to go along. At the same time, don't completely cut yourself off from the pain of your own truth. Sometimes, as a caller during a radio show once made clear, it's that very pain that may speak your love most clearly.

The natural, emotional trauma of watching someone you love die can be excruciating. Some respond by pushing even harder against the sun, demanding that the survivor try this or go there. Sadly, the person dying now is burdened with this support person's needs. Sadder still is the pain of the person who clutches with fear to the one dying until the very end.

Death and Fear

Say goodbye to each other with as much grace as possible while you still have the chance. Of course there can be fear and sadness. It's real to let that be known. But consider suspending those emotions in the final hours so you may be reunited in the love that held you together in life. If you battle against the sun to the very end, you leave little room for an honest goodbye. Your spirit is unavailable to the spirit of your loved one because it is occupied by fear. A final goodbye is powerfully painful. Fear makes it worse. Wouldn't you much rather release each other's hearts from this life with love?

There was a young woman in a group who had a great fear of death. She was devoted to her group for years. During that time she witnessed the dying of several group mates. Eventually, the young woman began missing group meetings because of her own illness, but she would always call to explain her absence. One week she didn't show for group, but there was no call. So someone in the group decided to call her and report back at the next session. At that next meeting the group found out the young woman had been raced to the hospital where she had nearly died.

The young woman eventually returned to her group. Everybody wanted to know what happened. It seemed some rare complication struck hard, and she was not expected to survive. Because the young woman had spoken at length about her fear of death in previous meetings, the group wanted to know what it was like for her to nearly die. Immediately, her arms went straight up over her head, hands wide open. Then, with a clear, quiet, soulful smile, and looking right into the heart of the group, she said, "Like letting go. Like putting your hands in the air at the top of the roller coaster." In that instant, death became something very different for the young woman and for each of us in her group.

Death for Tibetans brings with it what they refer to as a *Bardo*. According to this tenet, death creates for anyone involved an opportunity of tremendous spiritual movement. If hardship opens a window to greater truth, then death opens a door.

Chapter Twenty-Nine

Further Destinations: Matters of Spirit

Science and Matters of Spirit

Albert Einstein's work described the relationship between time, space, and energy, and concluded that it's all "relative." Interestingly, an experiment conducted by the HeartMath Institute suggests there is a cell in the human heart that, indeed, operates outside time and space. That cell, in essence, predicts the future. This experimental conclusion not only gives evidence to the notion that energy connects all things, but begins to provide proof of intuition.

In the experiment, human subjects were monitored for heart rate, respiratory rate, blood pressure and brain activity among other parameters. In the video detailing this research, *The Living Matrix-The New Science of Healing,* you can see countless wires attached to the people in the study.[23] The subjects are seated in front of a computer monitor, and shown a different image every eight seconds. The images fall into two distinct categories: those that produce a relaxation reaction and those that produce a fear reaction.

What the study found is truly astonishing. Simply put, an instant before an image was randomly flashed on the computer screen in front of the person being studied, that person's body reacted in a way consistent with the image that was *about to appear.*

If a disturbing image was flashed, there was a fear reaction, just before the image hit the screen. If a soothing image was randomly introduced, the body had a relaxation reaction before the image appeared. In other words, the body of the person being tested somehow knew before the image hit the screen, that the image was going to be disturbing or comforting. And guess where the reaction started? In the heart! The heart's reaction then triggered the brain that produced reactions in the rest of the body. The study seems to be suggesting what societies for eons have believed—we know things in our heart first. Some call this intuition.

You may have heard of Lawrence Anthony, the legendary author and conservationist also known as The Elephant Whisperer. He lived with a herd of elephants for years, studying their behavior and working to modify their habits that had gotten them into trouble with villagers who were threatening to kill off the herd. The Elephant Whisperer's devotion saved the animals.

Eventually the Elephant Whisperer left the herd to live with his family. When he later died, what followed amazed the world. Elephants are known to ritualistically grieve the death of their loved ones. Upon the death of the Elephant Whisperer, two wild herds he had lived with and saved began a twelve-hour trek across Africa, one arriving a day after the other. When finding his home, they filed passed it, then milled somberly in mourning. How did they know where he lived? How did they know he had died?

A final striking example of the energy web is evidenced by the work of Princeton researchers. In their 2002 article published in the *Journal of Scientific Exploration*, titled, "Coherent Consciousness and Reduced Randomness: Correlations on September 11, 2001," researchers reported how Random Event Generators (REGs) provided unprecedented and unintentional data from around the world.[24]

REGs are machines equipped to print random number sequences. Early research with REGs found that trained study participants could influence the pattern of numbers these machines printed without any physical or electronic connection to the devices. They did it with focused mental energy. Larry Dossey, MD, has written a captivating book called *Healing Words: The Power of Prayer and The Practice of Medicine*, which meticulously documents some of these early research projects.[25] With such remarkable results, other experiments were conducted. Over time, REGs were set up around the world, and allowed to run continuously.

All over the world, REGs were operating to produce printed records of random number patterns. And then it happened: September 11, 2001. In the days leading up to the catastrophic events of that day, REGs around the world began to record statistically significant less-random number sequences, with most machines spiking that change on the day of the tragedy.

The research makes it hard to think this is coincidence. Perhaps it's just the truth according to modern physics. Many cultures didn't and still don't need modern physics to support their ancient and continued practices that reflect these newly-researched phenomena. Fortunately for cultures like ours, modern physics is opening us back up to these possibilities.

Science, Death and Hope

In the last chapter, we introduced a Tibetan notion called the Bardo, the opening to matters of spirit for anyone exposed to a death experience. Death has been a regular part of my work with the chronically and terminally ill. Many illness survivors have allowed me into the final days of their journey. Many caregivers have let me stand beside them as they made their way beyond the death of the one they loved. These times have always engendered a deep stirring in some mysterious place in me, a place we all have.

It would be impossible for any person profoundly connected to another person by pain and honesty and hope and courage and real joy not to be moved by that person's death. This isn't about feeling the dying person's pain or getting lost in the loss. When repeatedly a part of this life/death dynamic, professionals' beliefs and values are often greatly affected. Curiously enough, great hope may be gleaned from these encounters.

Three of the most well-known contemporary experts in the mysteries of death and dying have found hope laced through their work. Raymond Moody, Jr., MD, PhD, Brian L. Weiss, MD, and the late Elisabeth Kubler-Ross, MD, all have ascribed to the belief that when the body dies the spirit lives on in a most favorable way.

More recently, the work of Anita Moorjani and Pim van Lommel, MD, shed fascinating light on near death experiences (NDEs).[26, 27] NDEs most commonly occur in patients declared clinically brain-dead and may include seeing oneself from a perspective above the body, feeling unconditional love from a being of light and taking part in a non-judgmental life review.

Dr. Van Lommel, a cardiologist, is the first to conduct a prospective and longitudinal study on NDEs. In his book, *Consciousness Beyond Life: the Science of the Near-Death Experience,* Dr. Van Lommel addresses many of the conventional explanations for NDEs including oxygen deprivation, seizure, psychological distress, birth memory, dreams, medication, etc. Two data points stand out from his research of those who met the strict criteria to qualify as a survivor of a NDE: this population reported their remembrance of the experience years later nearly identically to the first report, and made significant life changes, unlike those patients who reported NDE-like experiences but did not meet the NDE criteria.[28]

Moreover, the writings of Anita Moorjani and Dr's Moody, Weiss, and Kubler-Ross, among others, all conclude that the state of existence we come to after we leave the body is filled with truth and love. Many go on to say that we come to know an experience of unconditional regard beyond our grandest imaginations.

These hope-filled conclusions are the product of thousands of interviews these experts conducted with individuals who had NDEs. For Dr. Weiss, his conclusions come from regressive hypnotherapy with countless clients.

In one of his many books, *Through Time Into Healing*, Dr. Weiss writes, "It is important to keep an open mind, to trust your experiences. Don't let the dogma and beliefs of others undermine your personal experience and perceptions of reality."[29]

What Death and Dying Teach Us About Life

Much has been written about death and dying. The written word can teach, but experience changes everything. With enough experiences about life and death that go beyond what can be known with the mind, beliefs shape themselves. Life changes. Life expands.

This happened to Dr. Weiss, as described in his groundbreaking first book, *Many Lives, Many Masters*.[30] It also happened to acclaimed author Dr. Wayne W. Dyer, following his unconventional treatment for leukemia. I will always remember the first time I saw light around a dying person, a young man in his early thirties. He had been away from his weekly support group for a while because he was so sick. He came back to say goodbye. A beautiful, soft light was apparent around him. He died in love the next week. Days later, I was struck by the same light around a baby. It dawned on me that the baby had just come from the light, and the young man was being drawn back into it. The great poet William Wordsworth tells us, "Heaven lies about us in our infancy!"[31] That exclamation point is his.

Many caregivers have returned to their groups reporting that their dying loved one was heard talking with deceased friends and family members, reaching for them, or asking others in the room if they had seen these visitors. This is consistent with the findings of Dr. Moody and others. Many surviving near-death experiences report being greeted upon their own death by loved ones who have died before them.

Other mystical experiences are not uncommon for the dying. A lovely woman was nearing death, but still attending her weekly support group. One day in group, she began to stare up, moving her head as if tracking something high above her.

"What do you see?" I quietly questioned. The group was a bit taken aback by her behavior.

With an ever-so-slight smile she softly answered, "Eagles."

"Eagles carry the medicine of Great Spirit, according to Native American tradition," I offered. Her smile widened, and later she shared how comforted she was by the Native American belief. She died the next week.

With the gift of having traveled beside hundreds of survivors and caregivers, over miles and miles of roads on the illness journey, it is difficult not to see all as holy. Even death. We do our best to push against death and pain of all kinds. Yet, pain is firmly rooted in the human condition. It is hard to communicate how much *life* pours from rooms filled with illness survivors and caregivers, many in real pain or dying. These people come to these rooms with all their pain and all their hope and all their fear and all their courage. There, in that way, truths appear. In facing death, many see life for the first time.

Even death can give life. I remember a middle-aged man who was dearly loved by his group. Having missed many meetings without word from him or his family, the group believed he had died. We then spent the better part of a session saying goodbye, without him present. Each member, in turn, expressed what the man had meant to him or her. Much rich emotion and honesty rose up from the group. It was real. It was powerfully alive.

The next week, oxygen in tow, the man returned to the group. The group was awestruck. He, too, had come back to say goodbye. The group proceeded to say to him directly what had been said in his absence the week before. With the dying man's permission, each group member spoke to him from a place deep inside. Then the man spoke, eye to eye, with each group member. This was a divine moment. After addressing each of his fellow members individually, he spoke to the group as a whole: "I've waited all my life to know I meant something to someone. Now I know I do."

Near the close of this most poignant meeting, the man apologized to the group for exposing them over the last few months to the details of his dying, which included all sorts of practical questions and ethereal concerns. The group did a direct and effective job of releasing the man from his concern. Then the words of a very young member made their way straight to the heart of this matter: "Your journey has shown me sign posts along the way of death, so when that time comes for me, I will be more ready. Your grace in dying has given me hope."

After the meeting, I was debriefing with a young co-leader—someone who had been personally struggling with questions of religion and spirituality. With eyes wet, the young therapist said gently, "God was in there." I couldn't agree more.

Not only did dying not diminish the presence of love in these weekly support groups, it was in the very tension, torment, and truth of the dying process that I witnessed many *gaining* on life. This gain occurred not just with the dying members, but also with the surviving group members who saw more clearly what held value in the human experience through the dying and deaths of those they had grown so intimately connected.

Love never dimmed. That's not to say that group members were willing to face the death of their group mates with arms open. For sure it was hard. But even that expression of emotion was love and real and holy as well. Love cannot be bested by pain or death.

Shaped by these experiences, witnessing the death process time and time again, something changes inside. Seeing so much light coming from and through the journey of dying, the darkness our culture ties to death gets released. Life and death become different parts of the same wave. When deeply rooted in the security of this knowing, those of us still in body are empowered to branch further into all that human *life* offers. We know humanity, pain, confusion— we know darkness—to value the light. Cultures that embrace death and dying, rather than push against it, live with balance. Farmers understand this, exposed every year to the cycles of life.

Having been so shaped by experience, I am filled with broadened views. I believe that the most important part of each of us lives on beyond the physical form. This brilliant essence (call it the Self or the Soul) is evolving through life in each of us. In our purest form, we are compassion. We come to human life by choice and as an act of compassion. There is a most holy Source Of All compassion, and each of us is a glimmering facet of that Source—one with It, yet separate. As such, each of us created the blueprint for this life before we came, not God or our parents or anyone else.

We, like moths, seek more light. The world is a place to find out about light, truth, love. To find what expands love and what contracts it. With this developing awareness, our light grows. Soul growth is instinct in its highest form. Through life, we grow into as much of who we really are as possible. Even more of who we really are will become visible later.

Could it be that each person involved with the hardship journey chose that road, as a compassion-filled soul, before birth, through an act of love and desire for deeper understanding? Did the one suffering the most take on the most challenging part? Has each person in the journey evolved as a spiritual being? Through this united gesture of souls, have all those connected to the journey beyond hardship offered powerful and healing knowledge to all others?

Hardship opens the individual (as human and soul) to things before unseen, unfelt, and unknown. Collectively, this is power for transformation. Might it be so that all the people with all the horrible tragedies have been changing the world through their pain? Is this dynamic at work in all life journeys, whether painful or joyful? And what if death was simply a transition, not an opponent to be beaten? Where would we put all the joy and the hope and the peace? In the human experience, journey is the destination. Journeying is life. The human experience is part of the soul's journey. What if all this is part of the greater journey of mankind?

CHAPTER THIRTY

The Wheels of Hope

Hope and Expectation

Hope's a curious thing, isn't it? But what is it exactly? Most say hope is a feeling. Yet we often treat hope like it was more of a thing: "You need to get more hopeful," or, "I need to find a more positive, hopeful attitude." As if hope were a loaf of bread you picked up at the corner market. But hope seems to have a mind of its own, coming in random waves or cycles, like a wheel.

When asked about hope, most of us respond with ideas about something we want: "I hope to find work I love," "To meet my soul mate," "To have peace in the world," "To be more comfortable with myself." These are all honorable and reasonable wishes. And it does seem true that holding these wishes helps—*except when it doesn't.* So when can holding a good wish inside not be helpful? Let's take a look.

I love motorcycles. Many have ridden on the seat behind me. Each has a unique style back there, and always a joy. But one passenger in particular struck me with her manner. She was completely taken by this experience, though she had never ridden at highway speeds. I could hear her squeals of delight through both our helmets.

Totally pumped, in raw and unbridled enthusiasm as we snaked through an awesome countryside, she donned a kind of racer mode. The whole experience was a rush. To my amazement, as I laid us deep into a left sweeper, there was her face cradled in the crease of my left arm.

In corners like this, most new riders freak as the bike essentially "falls" into the turn. With this feeling of falling, new riders pull back and away. Not this woman. She leaned in even more.

I was laughing and twisting all at once. Her heavy anticipation of the turn, with its concurrent shift in body weight, changed the course of our cornering. Just like that, her anticipation had us heading for the ditches, forcing me to quickly snap my weight in the opposite direction, where the bike followed.

If we lean too heavy on our hopes and wishes with the weight of outcome expectations, we change the course of things, and actually steer ourselves away from where we want to go. This then is when holding a good wish inside may not be helpful.

But like a smooth roll through a perfect corner, it's the subtle balance between *leaning in a little and letting go* that gets us there. We lightly hope, or anticipate positively where we'd like to go, then allow things to take their own course. *Leaning in, letting go.* This is how to invite hope.

When you've got nine hundred pounds of iron between yours legs, you have to let that weight finds its own way. Life can sometimes be heavy. If you try to push it, that weight will turn on you. What most folks don't realize is that when you corner a big bike, there's no real steering: just leaning. You let the bike follow its natural inclination: the rider surrenders to the forces of gravity and the bike gracefully finds a fall line around the bend. Riding like this is virtually effortless, and things happen as they should. This is life. The fine balance between pointing things in the direction of what you want and hope for, but allowing all forces involved to be a part of that process so the weight of your expectations doesn't actually throw it all off course.

This begins to tease out the subtle difference between seeing something good happening in your mind's eye as if it were true, and expecting something. Expecting something is more a product of fear. Seeing something good as if it has already happened is more a product of love.

Paying Attention to What We Want

If we pay close attention, just beneath the surface of our hopes resides our fear. What we hope for is so often the polar opposite of what we fear the most. If I hope to be more comfortable with myself, there's a good chance I'm afraid I never will be. If I hope to be in less pain, could be I'm afraid the pain I'm in now won't get better.

This fear beneath our hope can blind us. If the gravity of my expectation to be more comfortable with myself or have less pain is so heavily attached to that outcome, I might miss those moments when I am in less pain, or am more comfortable with myself.

It's like I'm working so hard to feel better that I miss the things that actually do make me feel better. Consequently, I stay the troubled course. I keep heading away from what I hope for—heading for the ditches, if you will.

Speaking of ditches, one last motorcycle story. A friend told me he was driving near Branson, MO. While waiting to cross a two-lane highway, he witnessed something really scary, but very revealing. One of the cars ahead of him pulled out to cross the highway, not seeing an oncoming motorcycle. The crossing car tried to shoot across the road, but the motorcyclist locked his brakes and skidded right into the car.

No fun to report, but what was revealed in the accident has stuck with me. My friend said the skid marks left by the motorcycle actually curved right into the car. In other words, had the motorcyclist actually continued straight in the direction he was heading, he would have missed the car. If we fix our eyes on what we want to avoid, our body takes us right there. We wind up hitting what we wished to miss. Our body follows our eyes. That simple.

Fear keeps us looking at what we don't want: "Oh no, I'm gonna hit that car! I don't wanna hit that car!" Boom. "Oh no, I'm gonna spend the rest of my life miserable! I don't wanna be forever miserable!" Boom.

Train your attention on what you want.

The Science of Gathering Hope

Science tells us that the more we **lean in** and **let go**, the easier it is to do again. Here's how that works. First of all, when we are peaceful, joyful, hopeful, etc...the body produces a cascade of feel-good hormones. In those hormones are feel-good neuropeptides which act like little keys. These little keys then find their way to little keyholes on the surface of every cell, called neuroreceptors.

The more the little feel-good keys from the feel-good hormones fit in the little feel-good key holes, the better we feel. And the more time we spend feeling "good," the more feel-good keyholes are produced on the surface of our cells.

Second of all, the same thing happens when we feel sad or scared or hopeless. We produce more feel-bad hormones, feel-bad neuropeptide keys and neuroreceptor key holes. So the more we feel bad, the more feel-bad key holes cover the surface of our cells.

But here's the kicker. If we feel hope, peace, or joy a lot, cell surfaces are covered with feel-good key holes. So when the feel-bad keys show up, there's virtually no place for them to lock in. Result: the sadness doesn't stick, literally. Therefore, it becomes physically harder to feel bad and easier to feel good.

There ya go. The more hopeful we feel, the harder it is to be sad. We are gathering hope. How cool is that? There's more. Yes, way.

The more hope we feel, the more *neuropaths* are laid in the brain to carry hope's charge or frequency. So when the electric impulses related to fear or sadness get sent to the brain, there are limited paths for those charges to travel. Those roads aren't on the map. Therefore, those charges of difficult emotions dissipate more quickly than the charges of hope. But when the charges of hope, trust, love, etc., surge in the brain, bam…it's go time. Once again, hope is gathered.

Speaking of roads, how about this beautiful saying by philosopher, Lin Yutang: "Hope is like a path on the hillside. Once there was no path, but as villagers traveled that place, a way appeared."

He's speaking our language. Just as a path appears on the hillside when repeatedly traveled, the science of hope tells us that a path appears in the brain when we repeatedly think or feel a certain way. In other words, if you feel sad a lot, or hopeful a lot, pathways (called neuropaths) appear in the brain to support that hope or that sadness. And the more you walk that path, the more clear the path becomes, whether a path of hope or fear.

It's vitally important that you travel with compassion for yourself, whatever path. If you are struggling to feel strong and hopeful, as strange as it may sound, bring love to yourself then. Love yourself as best you can in the struggle. Otherwise, you are strengthening the neuropaths for fear and sadness. There's nothing wrong with difficult thoughts and feelings. You're having them for a reason. It's OK.

These are compassionate thoughts about your self. These thoughts produce love and trust in you. When you punish yourself for difficult thoughts, you actually produce more difficult thoughts and more feel-bad hormones.

What you want instead are thoughts that comfort and care for you: "I know I'm afraid of (fill in the blank) right now. OK. But that just gets me upset. It makes me hurt. I hurt enough already. I'm gonna think instead that things are gonna work out. That thought feels better."

This is compassionate change. The beauty of it is that you are not denying the difficult thoughts. You are actually acknowledging them, going through them, and coming out the other side.

This is also *leaning* with hope and *letting go* with trust. By so doing, you are not only strengthening your cells and neuropaths in the direction you want. You are lengthening the cycles and waves of your hope, gathering as you go. The wheels on the hope go round and round.

CHAPTER THIRTY-ONE

Bon Voyage

When writing, it seems there's a kind of connection made between you, the reader, and me. In a sense, we've covered some ground together. At the start of the trip, there was packing away tough emotions, then leaving home — leaving the familiar life you knew before your hardship hit. Once on the road to recovery from your hardship, it was about navigating the potholes, detours and traffic jams often caused by unexpected emotions, strained relationships, and serious bouts with big, tough feelings. Along the way there was some unpacking, to make room for emotions that gave you energy. In the end, there's always the hope of coming back to who you really are — the true Self. Welcome home.

But like all shared journeys, there's a goodbye. And out of respect for our time together, it seems right there be a fitting adios for us, too. The following account was written by a woman who came to counseling after a series of hardships. It represents much of what we've explored together, so with it I bid you bon voyage:

Growing up, I believed a broken heart was just part of the drama of romance gone wrong. Gratefully, that was all I knew when I was young.

My first true heartbreak came when my daughter was 4 months old and diagnosed with a rare genetic disorder. I was given something to read that said, "Severe psycho-motor retardation." The words burned a hole in my brain. There was some numbness, but it was soon replaced by fear, insecurity and a pain I could actually feel in my heart. And it hurt so much I didn't know how I would ever go on.

The world I grew up in didn't have room for people with disabilities. They were invisible, and even worse, mistreated. I was fearful for the life of our little girl, for her brother and for us. My hopes and dreams for her felt like they had been ripped out of me. I mourned the loss.

But I did go on. With the help of my husband, we connected to resources every way we could, learning about disability rights and the fight for dignity and inclusion. And my heart mended as we advocated and saw her flourish with options we helped create for her in school and the community. Our work for her even led me to a full-time career in parent education assisting other families of children with disabilities.

More pain and heartache came in the next years with alcoholism and 12-step programs, my mother's long and painful death, and my father coming to live with us in hospice before his death.

A year after I lost my father came a most unimaginable heartbreak. The boy I'd met in 6th grade and dated for 10 years, my husband of 35 years, died suddenly on his way home from work. His heart gave out at 58. And mine broke once again. I felt very alone, very old, very tired. Again, I didn't know how I would ever go on. My partner in all the past grief now was the one I was mourning.

Sudden loss. No time for denial. I was smacked with pain and reality and I couldn't hide. And this time I had a 23-year-old daughter to take care of alone, I thought. But our son, who had been living on the west coast, moved back home to help his sister and me. His longtime girlfriend, soon to be his wife, joined us. For eight months, until they moved into their own home, we held on to each other and we grieved.

It was a precious gift to have them with us, but there was no escaping the pain. The memories made me ache, but I also didn't want to forget. It was my only way out, to keep going through it. And it took so long.

Two years after my husband's death I knew I no longer could take care of my daughter. Despite all the help I had put together to support her, I was falling apart. The irony was we had always dreamed she would live on her own one day, as independently as possible. But, it was so hard to let go. It was more loss, and more heartbreak.

Loving deeply, I grieved deeply. Pain and fear were with me constantly. Anxiety ruled.

But like the heartbreak before, I again found myself drawn to an insatiable search for whatever I needed, this time to survive. I delved into the unknown, wanting to know everything about death, near death experiences, beliefs about the afterlife. I looked for my husband everywhere, in everything, seeking ways to make some sense of my new world. I was drawn into places that made me uncomfortable, doing things I had never done before.

After two unhappy attempts, I found the perfect therapist, a true spirit guide for my life. I read book after book and they became my support groups. I scoured the internet, attended seminars, watched movies and documentaries to explore topics I'd never had an interest in before. I did meditation, yoga, Healing Touch and Reiki energy work, hypnosis for past life regression – learning how to breathe, quiet my mind, and desperately try to stay in the moment.

I attended grief support groups, gave in and went on a medication for anxiety, talked to a religious leader about the afterlife. I connected with others to know I wasn't alone - amazing people who became the gifts of my life. Searching always, not only for my lost love, but for a me I could be at peace with — and love.

After fighting (with myself) to understand my early past, one that had seemed so full of love, but also, I discovered, had real danger, I began to feel and face my fears and anger. And it helped still the pain. I found a new quiet inside of me. And my heart began to repair, to open and trust again. I discovered what recovery meant for me:

Comfort and contentment from all the hard work and where it led me.
A more meaningful connectedness to others.
Peace from a new silence I so needed and welcomed.
Experiences of pure and simple joy I'd rarely experienced before.
Delight in "seeing" the serendipitous.
Gratitude I could actually feel in my mending heart.
A new spirit in my soul, safe in the knowledge that I always will be ok.

Am I fully aware all of the time of these newfound gifts?
A resounding no!
But I know they are there for me, they now are a part of me.

Hopeful, peaceful places deep inside I can connect to and make my heart feel full again.

When I finally began to feel better, I received this note from one of my closest friends (and also a beloved mentor):

"Just want you to know how I love watching, admiring and being in awe of your spirit shining and fighting through the hardest of times. It is so beautiful…it gives me joy, hope, faith, tears and smiles…know that I always carry you in my heart through all the suckiness and good times. I love your laugh! Celebrating your beauty…"

Amen.

References

1   Brydon, L., Walker, C., Wawrzyniak, A. J., Chart, H., Steptoe, A., "Dispositional optimism and stress-induced changes in immunity and negative mood," *Brain, Behavior, and Immunity.* 23(6): 810–816.

2   Kessler, R. C., McLeod, J. D., Cohen, S., Syme, S. L., "Social support and mental health in community samples," *Social Support and Health,* (San Diego, CA, US: Academic Press, 1985).

3   Vilhjalmsson, R., "Direct and indirect effects of chronic physical conditions on depression: A preliminary investigation," *Social Science and Medicine.* 47(5): 603–611.

4   Gruzehier, J.H., "A review of the impact of hypnosis, relaxation, guided imagery and individual differences on aspects of immunity and health," *Stress: The International Journal On the Biology of Stress,* 5(2): 147-163.

5   Mundy, E.A., DuHamel, K.N., and Montgemery. G.H., "The efficacy of behavioral interventions for cancer treatment-related side effects," *Seminars in Clinical Neuropsychiatry,* 8(4): 253–275

6   Watson, K., "A Better Argument-Without Getting Angry," *Natural Health,* Nov- Dec, 1998.

7   Salters-Pedneault, K., Tull, M. T., Roemer, L., "The role of avoidance of emotional material in the anxiety disorders," *Applied and Preventive Psychology,* 11(2): 95-114.

8   Rando, T.A., *Grief, Dying and Death: Clinical Interventions for Caregivers* (Research Press Company, 1985).

9   Figley, C.R., ed, *Compassion Fatigue: Secondary Traumatic Stress Disorders from Treating the Traumatized* (New York: Brunner/Mazel, Inc., 1995).

10 Bigatti, S.M., and Cronan, T.A., "An examination of the physical health, health care use, and psychological well-being of spouses of people with fibromyalgia syndrome," *Health Psychology*, 21(2): 157–166.

11 Morimoto, T., Schreiner, A.S., and Asano, H., "Caregiver burden and health-related quality of life among Japanese stroke survivors," *Age and Aging*, 32(2): 218–223.

12 Herbert, F., *Dune* (Philadelphia: Putnam, 1965).

13 Figley, *Compassion Fatigue: Secondary Traumatic Stress Disorders from Treating the Traumatized.*

14 Winston Churchill, Attributed. Quoted in Reader's Digest, Dec. 1954.

15 Hay, L.L., *You Can Heal Your Life* (Carlsbad, CA: Hay House, Inc., 1987), p. 219.

16 Lissoni, P., Cangemi, P., Pirato, D., Roselli, M.G., Rovelli, F., Brivio, F., Malugani F., Maestroni, G.J., Conti, A., Laudon, M., Malysheva, O., and Giani, L., "A review on cancer—Psychospiritual status interactions," *Neuroendocrinology Letters*, 22(3): 175–180.

17 Jawer, M. and Micozzi, M., *The Spiritual Anatomy of Emotion: How Feelings Link the Brain, the Body, and the Sixth Sense* (Rochester: Park Street Press, 2009).

18 Moorjani, A., *Dying To Be Me: My Journey From Cancer, To Near Death, To True Healing* (Carlsbad, CA: Hay House, Inc., 2012) pp. 145-146.

19 Genesis, *The Lamb Lies Down on Broadway* (UK: Charisma/Virgin, 1975).

20 Tolle, E., *A New Earth: Awakening to Your Life's Purpose* (New York: Dutton, 2005).

21 Huber, C., *There Is Nothing Wrong with You: Going Beyond Self-Hate* (USA: Keep It Simple Books, 2010).

22 Buhner, S., "How you really can listen with your heart," *Spirituality & Health*, 2012 Soul/Body Connection: 79–83.

23 *The Living Matrix-The New Science of Healing,* Greg Becker, Susan Becker, Harry Massey (2009; The Living Matrix, Ltd. and Becker Massey, LLC, dvd).

24 Nelson, R., "Coherent consciousness and reduced randomness: correlations on September 11, 2001," *Journal of Scientific Exploration*, 16(4): 549-570.

25 Dossey, L., *Healing Words: The Power of Prayer and The Practice of Medicine* (San Francisco: Harper San Francisco, 1993).

26 Moorjani, *Dying To Be Me: My Journey From Cancer, To Near Death, To True Healing.*

27 Van Lommel, P, *Consciousness Beyond Life: The Science of the Near-Death Experience* (New York: Harper One, 2010).

28 Van Lommel, *Consciousness Beyond Life: The Science of the Near-Death Experience.*

29 Weiss, B.L., *Through Time into Healing* (New York: Simon & Schuster, 1992), p. 42.

30 Weiss, B.L., *Many Lives, Many Masters: The True Story of a Prominent Psychiatrist, His Young Patient, and the Past-Life Therapy That Changed Both Their Lives* (New York: Simon & Schuster, 1988).

31 Quiller-Couch, A., ed, *The Oxford Book of English Verse: 1250-1900* (Oxford: Clarendon, 1919), 536.Ode.

Bibliography

- Borysenko, J., (audio cas.), *Healing and Spirituality: The Sacred Quest for Transformation of Body and Soul.* Carlsbad, CA: Hay House, 2000.
- "It's All Good Here," 2015, http://www.itsallgoodhere.com.
- Naparstek, B., (audio cas.), *Health Journeys: A Meditation for Relaxation and Wellness.* Cleveland: Image Paths, 2002.
- Moore, T., *Care of the Soul.* New York: HarperCollins, 1992.
- Perls, F.S., *Gestalt Therapy Verbatim.* Moab, UT: Real People Press, 1959.
- Weiss, B., *Messages from the Masters.* New York: Warner Books, 2000.
- Young, S., *Breakthrough Pain: A Step-by-Step Mindfulness Meditation Program For Transforming Chronic and Acute Pain.* Boulder, CO: Sounds True, Inc., 2004, cd.
- Zukav, G., and Francis, L., *The Heart of the Soul.* New York: Simon and Schuster, Inc., 2002.
- Dyer, W., *Wishes Fulfilled: Mastering the Art of Manifesting.* Carlsbad, CA: Hay House, Inc., 2012.

About the Author

Greg Pacini, a Licensed Professional Counselor and Certified Group Psychotherapist with 35 years experience, has conducted more than 3500 group therapy sessions for hardship survivors, parents, and physicians. He's a speaker, consultant, and psychotherapist in private practice providing dream work, spiritual quest support and help managing hardship, anxiety and depression. Visit him at www.gregpacini.com. Follow him on Facebook at Greg Pacini, Counselor, LLC.

Printed in the United States
By Bookmasters